AVID
READER
PRESS

THE ART OF WINNING

BILL BELICHICK

AVID READER PRESS

NEW YORK   AMSTERDAM/ANTWERP   LONDON   TORONTO   SYDNEY/MELBOURNE   NEW DELHI

AVID READER PRESS
An Imprint of Simon & Schuster, LLC
1230 Avenue of the Americas
New York, NY 10020

First Avid Reader Press hardcover edition May 2025

AVID READER PRESS and colophon are trademarks of Simon & Schuster, LLC

Interior design by Ruth Lee-Mui

Manufactured in the United States of America

1   3   5   7   9   10   8   6   4   2

Library of Congress Cataloging-in-Publication Data has been applied for.

ISBN 978-1-6680-8083-2
ISBN 978-1-6680-8085-6 (ebook)

To my mom, Jeannette, and my dad, Steve,
for their love and support.

To Bill Edwards, my godfather, and
my father's college and NFL coach.

My father's book, Football Scouting Methods, *was dedicated*
to Bill Edwards, but the dedication page was left out.
The Belichick family is forever indebted to Bill Edwards and
his wife, Dorothy, for inspiring three generations of coaches.

To my grandparents, Leslie and Irene Munn and
John and Mary Belichick, for the sacrifices they made for
their children, grandchildren, and future generations.

To my children, Amanda, Stephen, and Brian.
Your love and inspiration power our journey.
I have watched you grow as parents and as coaches.

CONTENTS

INTRODUCTION

This book will tell you how I did my job as a coach, coordinator, and general manager (without the title). Titles do not mean as much as your performance on the job. This book will also tell you how I did my job as an assistant, well before I could point to any sustained success in my career, because the foundation for success can be—and must be—built wherever you are, and in whatever role you have. Each person in an organization contributes to the success of the team.

I have been on ninety-seven sports teams in my life. Forty as a player, fifty-six as a coach, and the NFL 100 All-Time Team. I have learned from all of them.

Nineteen of the teams were before high school, and included basketball, softball, lacrosse, and football. My first basketball coach, Barry Carter, taught me about team defense, not scoring. My first softball coach owned a pharmacy in Annapolis called Carville's. He taught our team about sportsmanship. We always went to his soda fountain after our games and got snow cones. After one of our (few) losses, we did not give a good cheer and we did not go to Carville's. My 135-pound football coach, Richard Mann, ran the single wing. I am glad I played on that offense.

I played on ten teams in high school and eleven teams in college. Every year was a great learning experience. Al Laramore and Steve Sorota were great high school football coaches, but had very different coaching styles. I learned that both styles of coaching worked. Sorota, and my college lacrosse coach, Terry Jackson, gave the players a lot of responsibility on the field. I learned to do that when I became a coach. And I played one year of club lacrosse in Denver as a weekend warrior—playing on weekends without training was tough.

My coaching career in the NFL is well-documented. I also coached my sons' teams in lacrosse: Steve in Huntington, New York, with Scott DeMonte, and Brian in Weston, Massachusetts, with Matt Dwyer (and Brian's summer team, the Nor'easters). I learned that the rate of improvement with pre–high school players was much greater than with professionals.

Being part of the 100 All-Time Team, organized in 2019 on the hundredth anniversary of the league, was my biggest personal honor. The members of that team are elite—I idolized many of the players and coaches who were older than me. Those men were the stars when I first started watching and learning about football. I appreciated the contemporary players and coaches from competing against them. Walking onto the field before the Super Bowl in 2020 with the likes of Jim Brown, Lawrence Taylor, Tom Brady, and the rest of the 100 All-Time Team was the best feeling. What a team!

Finally, I want to acknowledge the 1963 Navy team, or "The President's Team," as author Michael Connelly calls it. Documentaries by Jack Ford and Pete Radovich have captured moments about this special group of players and coaches. Admiral Tom Lynch captained the team, which still remains very close today. As a head football coach, I have always wanted my team to play and act like the 1963 Navy team: tough, smart, dependable, unselfish. I never dreamed my team would have a Hall of Fame quarterback like Roger Staubach, but we did—Tom Brady. We also had leadership comparable to Tom Lynch. I was touched by Lynch's offer to be an honorary member of his team.

At the beginning of my coaching career, I wasn't just at the bottom of the ladder, I wasn't even *on* the ladder. I was underground, but I was observing, and learning.

Eventually, I got a spot on the bottom of the NFL ladder and began to climb. Along the way, I learned from hundreds of players, coaches, scouts, and other associates on four different teams before I became a head coach in Cleveland. I also learned a lot from studying my opponents—nothing forced me to improve more than strong competition. I learned from victories, from losses, and from my many mistakes. Through it all, I never stopped learning and working to produce better results.

As your job or role in life changes, you have to evolve and adjust too. I hope that this book will help you improve your performance, wherever you happen to be on the ladder.

I was born into football. For years my father, Steve Belichick, was an assistant coach at the Naval Academy, and by all accounts, he was the best game scout anyone had ever seen. I grew up immersed in preparation as I watched my father scout opponents. I learned how to watch a game, how to break down film, how to find keys and tips for players to use in the game, and how to gain an advantage by studying opponents' tendencies. I still use these techniques.

For the last half century, I have been a coach. I have never stopped learning about the game and learning about competition. I have learned about what makes human beings excel and what makes human beings *want* to excel. I have led men through months of mental and physical preparation, and then into months of the most intense athletic competition in the history of the world. The game of football combines hand-to-hand combat with circus-like acrobatics, and coaching the game demands complex strategic planning—and success in the game requires the highest commitment from its players, coaches, and staff.

As I began to succeed as a coach, first in New York and then in New England, I started to establish in my mind a series of principles, rules of thumb, habits, and philosophies that I understood to be fundamental to our teams' successes. When we won, I kept what worked. When we lost, I threw out what hadn't. Over time, these ideas coalesced into a single, coherent program. But that was only half the battle. If my program—or any program—were to ever have any chance of success, it would have to be communicated to hundreds of people with unique personalities, who came from all walks of life and were in possession of a wide range of different skills. Those people would have to unite under one vision, coordinated to seek one goal. Happily, my program works, and I can communicate it. The proof of that is in the record books.

In a game as competitive as football, you might be surprised to see a practitioner decide to share secrets of his trade. But it happens. In fact, my father did it, in 1962, with *Football Scouting Methods*, a now-classic book on the subject. Generations of scouts have made use of his methods. Football has been very good to me and my family—spanning three generations. I am inspired to write this book partly because of what he did, and partly because I would like to give back to the game that has done so much for me and three generations of my family. Giving back to the game has been something I have been committed to for a long time. I welcomed college and high school coaches to our spring practices in New England and I spoke annually at coaching clinics around the country, as far back as Frank Glazier's clinics in the eighties on the Jersey Shore. I attended the annual coaches' convention with my dad for years, and we would listen together to the top college coaches give clinic talks. (Although I probably learned more outside the lecture rooms, where I was able to listen in on conversations about everything from job hunting to proper stance technique, and every new play, idea, or training method that traveled through the hotel lobby.)

I hope that this book can give back some of what I have taken from football.

Besides my father's model, I was also inspired to write this book by Ray Dalio, the brilliant founder of Bridgewater and author of *Principles*. Although Ray seldom refers to football in his book, I found his book incredibly useful. I had opportunities to talk with Ray and he helped convince me to share my own principles, as he shared his. I am glad he did. By the way, I acknowledge right here that Ray has given me permission to borrow his term "principles," which I will use in this book. Principles are foundational pieces—pillars, if you will—upon which you will build your base for sustained success. Some are nonnegotiable and some are flexible. However you choose which principles are best for you, consistency in application will be critical to their working.

If a team cannot consistently do the most important things that correlate to winning, that team has no chance to win consistently. Almost every day of my coaching career, I have organized and prioritized my thoughts for that day—whether that involved talking to the team and staff, or summarizing evaluations on college players. Authoring a book allowed me to pull all these principles together on a large scale. Thank you, Ray.

And thanks to Jack and Suzy Welch for sharing their thoughts in our many football and business conversations. Jack and Suzy gave me so much insight on what the other side is thinking in business deals, and they helped me understand the four quadrants of employees, ranging from "Must keep them" to "Get rid of them ASAP": productive with a great attitude; productive with a bad attitude; not productive with a good attitude; not productive with a bad attitude.

Ultimately, my NFL career was centered on one thing, and only one thing: What can I do to help our team win? I learned the centrality of that question as a kid running around the facilities at Annapolis, listening and paying attention to my father and the other coaches. In high school I played, but I was never a great player. I did have the privilege to play for Al Laramore and the Annapolis High School Fighting Panthers. Coach Laramore was a legendary multisport coach in Maryland and had success at football, basketball, and lacrosse. His style reinforced many principles that I learned from my childhood observations of Navy football. First, anything that involved helping the team win was important, and other than family and academics, most everything that didn't relate to winning took a back seat. Second, hard work and conditioning were paramount—outworking your competition was absolutely a pillar of both programs. Third, discipline on the football field correlated to winning. In other words: don't beat yourself. Finally, everybody was replaceable. Anybody could be injured, so everyone had to be ready to do their job.

We're going to work, we're going to be disciplined, and it's going to be hard. Football is hard. Winning is hard. Life is hard and so is our program. It's demanding and it's not for everyone. Neither am

I. But to get to the top, and stay there, is close to impossibly hard. So we do hard things. Everyone wants something, but how much pain and sacrifice are you willing to endure to get it? That's the work part and that's part of a winning culture.

Above all, do not beat yourself—you cannot win until you keep from losing.

As a head coach, more often than not, helping the team win doesn't look warm and fuzzy. It looks like work—usually hard work—if you want to outcompete your opponent. In this book, I want to take the reader deep inside my coaching and leadership style and share what I have learned. My philosophy is what led to winning—winning didn't develop into a philosophy. My philosophy may surprise you at times. At other times it might seem almost strangely obvious. (My rule on how to win football games: score the most points. Job titles and likes on social media do not win football games.)

Finally, a lot has been made of the way I communicate with players in team meetings or with the media after games. It has been described in many different ways over the years—direct, constructive, scathing, educational. Occasionally entertaining, perhaps.

But this is my playbook. I'm not talking to any TV reporter, and I'm not in the middle of another season of football with its infinite exigencies and requirements on my time. Now I get to explain what I mean, and why I mean it. For many of the principles in *The Art of Winning* that I'll share with you, I'll also share stories to illustrate them. And I don't have to worry about my words getting clipped into a sound bite or twisted out of context.

ONE

BIG GAMES, BIG MOMENTS

Big games aren't different from any other games. But everything *around* big games is different. It's the same for big moments in any line of work. Fundamentally, your process for getting to the big moment is the process that is most likely to win the day. Don't get distracted by all the other stuff. Nevertheless, this is a chapter about all the other stuff, and how to deal with it.

It might seem strange to start the book here with the "final goal"—the culmination of all your work—but focusing first on that goal will ground and orient all the principles in this book and how you think about them. For us in football, the final goal is the Super Bowl. To win one, we must have a vision of what we're trying to accomplish, and we have to stick to that vision, no matter how many distractions are around. To win more than one, we have to realize

9

that a big win isn't the end of anything. It's the beginning of trying to win the next one.

You cannot think of big tests and triumphs as "final" in any respect. If you think about winning as something that starts and stops, something that can be turned on or off, or as something that can be "ramped up" when convenient, then you will never be ready to implement a true sustainable winning program. There are no end points in winning, period.

An NFL team plays seventeen regular-season games, and they're all highly consequential. You can't underperform for an entire regular season, get to the postseason, and declare "I'm ready." With that attitude, you'll never get there to begin with. To reach your ultimate goal, you cannot try to master a result. You must master a *process*. A good process results in good habits. Consistent good habits result in dependability. The goal is to have a good, consistent process—and good results will follow. Then, winning becomes a practice. And finally, a habit. In other words, when we prepare to win, we prepare to win all the time.

I understand that this might seem easier said than done. What about those moments at work when you pull something off, something big, and you get celebrated for it? You're supposed to just take that in stride? You work hard, you get recognized, and suddenly your boss hands you a big opportunity, a real chance to prove yourself, and you're *not* supposed to treat it as a big deal? How do you not feel a mixture of hype and dread about that? How many of those opportunities come up for any of us in our careers?

I get that. Just because I don't think about big moments this way doesn't erase a very human tendency to get panicked or excited when facing a big test. Plenty of players in the NFL operate that way too (believe me), and treating a big game as something separate from the rest of the season certainly isn't confined to football.

Have you ever gone out and bought new shoes or a new suit before a big day at work? Perhaps you were going to represent the company somewhere, or it was the first time back with your team after working remotely for a while. You want to make an impression, of course. It's natural. But then by lunch you have blisters because the shoes aren't broken in, or the suit jacket's too tight—and then you start thinking about rushing back home to get your old loafers, and you lose track of all your careful preparation.

Building a good process starts with identifying and understanding what is most important to success. Make sure to prioritize the major points for a successful process, and don't waste time and energy on stuff that doesn't really move the needle. A successful process depends on ignoring the noise.

And, unfortunately, the noise exists.

While I maintain that big games are no different from regular games, it is unavoidably true that what *surrounds* a big game sets it apart. There's a chaos that you need to meet and manage. That chaos can be a problem—but, like any problem, you can turn things around to your advantage by understanding what you need to focus on (and letting your opponents get distracted by the bright lights).

To manage the chaos around big moments you will need to call up your administrative and managerial skills, rather than anything dramatic or decisive. As a football coach, for every triumphant moment in the swirling confetti, there are ten thousand moments of quiet preparation. Big moments are won by winning all the small moments that come before them. And they're not all fun. Learn to embrace this kind of tedious detail work and you will be successful in your job, which will eventually lead to other opportunities and more responsibility.

Here's an example. The moment we win a conference championship game and advance to the Super Bowl, the Belichick Travel Agency opens. I wear many, many hats as a coach—organizer, motivator, amateur psychologist, disciplinarian, truth teller, accountant—and travel agent is one of them. The Super Bowl is a big, complicated affair, and I've got sixteen hundred tickets, three hundred hotel rooms, thousands of miscellaneous event tickets, and two planes' worth of family travelers to organize and distribute. Even though it's not my favorite part of the job, I do it with as much energy and attention as I can muster. These kinds of details are important to people, and for a brief time, I'm all ears. After that, we're all ball.

When the Belichick Travel Agency is open, I perform my role as energetically as I do any other part of my job. There's a time to say yes and there's a time to say no, and in the pursuit of sustained excellence, you're going to end up saying no a lot more than yes—so when I *do* say yes, I don't do it begrudgingly. I give people what they need so that we as a team get what we need later on, and what we need is for each player to play well and not be worried about making arrangements for his family. My job is to minimize (or eliminate) distraction so that each player can perform at his highest level. If I expect to be able to ask my slot receiver to play in a pinch at cornerback in front of a hundred million viewers on TV, I don't get to ignore his request for a hotel room with a nice view.

Dividing the inventory of tickets and prime travel positions isn't something I would ever hand off to an assistant or intern, at least not initially. It takes a steady hand to plan what amounts to a five-day party for hundreds of people. Everyone is already on edge from the competitive pressure of the upcoming game and from their phones, which have been exploding with congratulatory messages (and requests). You cannot ignore the frenzy and hope it will go away. Leaders adapt, and leaders do what needs to be done.

So, instead of being laser-focused on red-zone tendencies and takeaway opportunities, I'll spend some of my time and attention addressing hotel accommodations and ticket allotments and help my players' families and friends make arrangements to come and cheer us on. It might sound funny to be worrying about room sizes or complimentary breakfasts, but if it does, I'm guessing you've never performed your job in front of 125 million people. If you did, the people you love and who love you would also want to be there to support you, to show off their rightful pride. And you would want to help facilitate that. Is it ultimately a sideshow? Of course. But it doesn't feel like it to the guys who have worked as hard as they have to get to the biggest moment in their lives. As a leader, I can't look at the team and tell them they're wasting their time. So when those calls come in and a player's cousin is asking for a king over a queen bed, or an uncle is wondering what party he can get into, the Belichick Travel Agency policy is to give players the opportunity to answer. But we will do it on a clock.

Two days. That's how long we like to keep the agency open. And during that time, while I'm thinking about the players' accommodations, they are required to think about this question: In two months, two years, or twenty years from now, what part of this process will they remember? It won't be the size and spectacle, and it won't be whether they got a junior or full suite. The only thing anyone will remember is whether we won or lost.

To help them focus on what matters, I like to tell my players and coaches to think about "the drawer." Whether real or imagined, the drawer is the place where they can put every nonessential task, responsibility, and commitment so that their focus can be purely on doing their jobs. To be clear, I'm not telling them to throw anything away—it's a drawer, not a trash can—just place it somewhere safe that they can return to once the job is done. The drawer is a tool for managing distractions. It's also my way of acknowledging that we are all human, we are all pulled in different directions, and we are all imperfect—but we *can* make a choice to rise above that imperfection and those distractions, if temporarily.

It might sound simple, but it's effective. Really big moments are infrequent and nobody wants to look back with regret because they were distracted and didn't perform their best when it mattered most. You honor commitments by paying full attention to them, not by randomly swinging back and forth between what matters and what doesn't based on your mood or anxiety.

I am asking my players to honor their *current* commitment to win, while at the same time acknowledging the other obligations in their lives. There will be a time for the other stuff.

The drawer is a toolbox, something you can open and grab from when you need to. It's about adaptability (more on that later) and about awareness. Sometimes, a player might realize that they *can't* put something in there. If that happens, we deal with it. And we're better for it.

The day before the 2002 Super Bowl, downtown New Orleans had become an early Mardi Gras, jam-packed with people, fans, media, anyone trying to get close to the action—no place to sequester a team trying to concentrate on the upcoming game, much less walk through some plays. It became untenable, so early Saturday evening, we boarded buses for a nondescript and infinitely quieter hotel outside of town. It was perfect. Except for the fact that Adam Vinatieri had drawn the short straw and been placed in a smoking room. And man, had that room been smoked in. (It was 2002, it was New Orleans, and it was a hotel next to the airport. Use your imagination.) The stench was eye-watering. If we had been in "big game mode," Adam might have convinced himself that the stakes were too high to complain, or that it was something he could shove in the drawer. But instead, he knew what he needed to perform. So he spoke up about his accommodations, and the Belichick Travel Agency made a rare exception to act outside our stipulated operating hours and switched him to another room. He rewarded us the next day by kicking a fairly significant field goal. His win became our win.

Concepts like the drawer and the Belichick Travel Agency are ways I navigate the distractions surrounding big games. These techniques acknowledge reality, while at the same time emphasizing what our job really is. Without them, I'd just be hoping for the best. I'd have to bet on several dozen different people, all uniquely motivated, to remain focused during an unbelievably distracting time. I don't like those odds. Once players (and coaches) get distracted, they lose touch with the preparation that got them to the big moment in the first place. That's where losing begins. If distractions take over an event, and we lose, the results can never be reversed and we will all live with the outcome for the rest of our lives. I work hard to make sure that this doesn't happen, and we don't underperform.

Sometimes, the pressure and hoopla surrounding the Super Bowl can also cause some coaches (and certainly some players) to forget what got them there in the first place. When people get to the big game, they think they need to meet the moment by doing something dramatic. The thought process is like this: it's the biggest stage, so it's the time to pull out a new plan, a surprise play, something that's going to shock and awe. For example, instead of drinking one 5-Hour Energy drink, you might drink three to triple your energy. Take it from me: it doesn't work like that.

THE ART OF WINNING

We won our first Patriots Super Bowl in part because we *didn't* do anything we hadn't done before. People focus on the fact that we developed a new defensive game plan against the St. Louis Rams between the first time we played them that season and when we faced off in New Orleans for the championship, but what they forget is that we had also developed a new game plan against *every* team we played that year (and every team we would play during my entire time with the Patriots). It would have been a betrayal of the principles and practices that had brought our team to the Super Bowl if we had pumped the brakes and decided to "play it safe" by simply and passively replaying a game we had played before, especially considering the fact that the Rams had beaten us in the regular season—we couldn't be tempted to keep things the same, or fall back on what had already worked, because then we would just lose again. Consistency doesn't mean a resistance to change. It means commitment. And in our case, our commitment was to adapting. I was determined to treat the Super Bowl just like we treated every other game that season, and that meant we were going to adjust what we did on defense to what our opponent wanted to do on offense.

The Rams offense that year was truly special, and they did a great job of building it, coaching it, and winning with Kurt Warner, Marshall Faulk, and a wide receiver corps for the ages. So when they beat us in the regular season, it was frustrating. The final tally was 24–17—closer than it should have been, but we got a defensive touchdown on an interception return by our cornerback Terrell Buckley, meaning we scored only ten points on offense. Tom Brady was ineffective in that game, in large part because I gave him only half of his normal reps in practice that week (more on that later). On defense, I also made a major miscalculation by thinking we could disrupt the Rams' passing game by blitzing Kurt Warner with five-man pressures on over half the plays. The Rams blocked them cleanly. The only thing we ended up disrupting with our defensive plan was our own pass coverage, and Warner chewed us up. That game had one of the worst defensive game plans of my career.

My job as head coach is to give the players a chance to win. I have to provide them with a game plan and prepare them for their opponent. In the NFL, where the playing field is level, our game plans and preparation matter a lot, but ultimately the players have to go on the field and make the plays to win the game. Good players cannot overcome bad coaching. If I do not do my job, they cannot do theirs. In the regular season, I had done a poor job and we lost against the Rams. Two and a half months later, when we met again in the Super Bowl, we did what any winning team should do: we looked at our opponent, and we adapted to what we saw. It wasn't a "Super Bowl game plan" or a "kitchen sink game plan." Nothing special, nothing unique, nothing dramatic. Just the same strategizing and film study that we had done every other week that year, the same commitment to planning that had gotten us to where we wanted to be.

I'll say it again: not the same *plan*; the same *planning*.

In New Orleans, I did a better job of preparing the team than I had in the regular season (although the game still came down to the final play). Our game plan this time around was fundamentally different: we decided to give less attention to disrupting Warner and instead go after the lynchpin of their timing-based offense, Marshall Faulk, who was an extraordinary, multitalented back, capable of breaking off for huge gains as a runner or receiver. In concrete terms, we were going to weaken our front line in favor of beefing up our defensive backs. We ran plays with five, six, or even seven players in the secondary, a defense that I had first experimented with some years before with the Giants, when we were facing the legendary Barry Sanders, one of the most difficult running backs I have ever prepared against.

Not only did we try to contain Faulk, but also we shifted resources away from the front line (and from pressure on Warner) and toward disrupting wide receivers Torry Holt and Isaac Bruce. To be blunt: we physically harassed them on every step they tried to take. During the regular-season game, the trio of Holt, Bruce, and Faulk had combined for nearly three hundred receiving yards and two TDs. Perhaps even more significantly, Warner had targeted those three players twenty-eight times. If he felt any pressure from our defense that day, it didn't matter: he had plenty of star talents to target, and he did, and they won.

Ironically, by focusing on disrupting the receivers rather than putting pressure on Warner, we were actually able to get to Warner more because the receivers weren't able to run uncontested routes, and Warner had to hold the ball longer on pass plays. We blitzed less, but our smothering defense of his favorite targets ended up disrupting their overall timing and we got more sacks—and one franchise-changing pick-six by Ty Law.

So, to sum up, our two areas of focus in that 2002 Super Bowl were: (1) to be extremely physical with the Rams' explosive receivers; and (2) to attack Marshall Faulk wherever he went. Tactically, this meant that instead of bringing five or six defenders at Warner when he dropped back (as we did during the regular-season matchup), we sent those defenders after his targets. It worked out for us, and we won.

Well, it worked out for *most* of us.

Before each of the Patriots' nine trips to the Super Bowl, I delivered the same cautionary message to our team and staff: This is a business trip. We aren't fans, and we're here to do our jobs. If you want to soak in the atmosphere and the hoopla, buy a ticket and enjoy. You have the rest of your life to experience Super Bowl week as a fan. But when we're there as a team, *we* are the show and the rest of the circus is for everyone else. Sure, there will be a little social time for family and friends, but in every other step of the week leading up to the game, we should focus on our preparation and our readiness to perform at our highest level.

And that means: *there are no guests in your hotel room.* To be clear, that rule goes for training camp and regular-season road trips, and it certainly applies at the Super Bowl. No friends, wives, girlfriends, agents, cousins. If you want to see someone in a hotel room, go somewhere else. I could not have been more direct about it, during my entire career.

Unfortunately, two nights before the 2002 Super Bowl, a player had a female friend in his room. Although he wasn't going to play in the game anyway, he still wasn't going to get away with this indiscretion. So I sent him home.

Think of how embarrassing that must have been.

There he was, with his team at the biggest game in the world, the pinnacle of professional sports, a lifelong dream for every football player . . . and he had to return home the day before the game, while his family and friends were still in town. For the rest of his life, every time that Super Bowl is mentioned, or a highlight is shown, he'll think about not having been there (and he'll think about why he wasn't there). By getting caught up in non-football stuff, he made a bad decision, took a risk, rolled the dice—and lost. It wasn't a total loss, to be fair. We won the game, and he got his Super Bowl ring. As a team, we also got a good cautionary tale going forward. Rules and expectations are not hollow. They're at the foundation of how any winning team must operate.

• • •

Dwelling on all the bright lights and distractions surrounding big moments sets us up for failure, because it takes us away from winning habits. All the hype reorients our focus on things that don't have to do with winning (such as "legacy"). And that's when people start playing selfishly and stupidly. It's critical to remind people of this. Collectively as a team, we need to do everything together and support each other.

Before every game in the regular season leading up to the 2002 Super Bowl, our team walked out of the tunnel as one. It was just what we did. But four days before the Super Bowl, an NFL game operations representative got in touch with us about the league's final preparations with the pregame script and timeline—did we want our starting offensive or defensive players to be announced as we took the field? I told my colleague Berj Najarian to tell them, "Neither." Our entire team would come out as a group, as it had all season long. On the Friday before the Super Bowl, when word of my answer had spread, a league representative called and told me this wouldn't work. He said that we all had a very strict schedule, that the Super Bowl was a television product of astonishing complexity, and that it was critically important that we all follow the script: eleven starters for each team had to be announced individually during a period of time not to exceed one minute and forty seconds. With this additional pushback from the league and network, I revisited the decision with our captains to make sure that the team was still on board with the plan. The captains agreed that we should come out as a team.

We would come out as we had been coming out, in the way that had gotten us, as a team, to this moment: instead of having eleven starters trotting out one at a time as our opponent did, all forty-five

Patriots poured onto the field as one entity far stronger than the sum of our individual parts.*

It's a widely celebrated decision now, but there was no guarantee that it would be received warmly in the moment.

Athletes dream their whole lives about running out onto the field, hearing their name announced to the world amid as much pageantry as possible. For a few precious seconds, a global spotlight was set to be trained on them alone. But our group of players decided to forgo that individual glory in favor of the collective. That is real sacrifice and a real commitment to winning. Some of those players would go on to become immortal in their own right and have careers that would afford them dozens or hundreds of opportunities to be globally recognized. For many others, that was their one moment in the spotlight.

On TV, Pat Summerall described to millions of people all over the world how, "instead of being introduced individually, as is the tradition in Super Bowls, the team [is] coming out en masse as the Patriots . . ." His partner John Madden added: "Showing the unity that this team has shown all season long." If we hadn't already been doing that group introduction all season, and if we hadn't all bought into a team-first identity, and if we hadn't really committed to all doing our jobs together, it would have meant nothing. People would have thought it was just a PR stunt. But the work we did before the big game made it possible for us to exploit all the hoopla and recommit to our fundamental principles. For years, people have told me they rooted for the Patriots because of that one image. We shared equally in what became a much greater moment than we

---

* The moment was indeed very powerful, but, sure enough, the timing ended up being awkward. They weren't kidding about that minute and forty seconds—after our initial group introduction, we stood on the field looking a little lost and waiting for the signal to head to the bench.

even imagined. And for the rest of our lives, we can lay claim to having participated in the most famous Super Bowl introduction of all time. Who would get the credit? Nobody cared. In the process, everyone shared it.

I cannot say it enough times: my job is to prepare the team to win, and a big part of my job is to have the players in the right frame of mind for the game. In the 1997 Super Bowl, when I was an assistant under Bill Parcells, the Patriots played the Packers in New Orleans and the players had a meeting the *night before the game* about who would be introduced during the broadcast. Yet another distraction, and one that could have been avoided entirely. Our team introduction in 2002 eliminated the need for a (potentially explosive) meeting so close to the kickoff.

Years later, in another Super Bowl, we experienced a uniquely annoying distraction. Swag ("stuff we all get") is a part of being in the NFL. We would get more gear—more apparel, sneakers, hats, duffel bags—than we knew what to do with. Some of the stuff really was useful (I have several worn-out hoodies that I would wear daily), but plenty just got packed away and mostly forgotten. At big games, pro and college, one of the perks is the heightened quality and sheer amount of swag for players. Electronics, headphones, gift cards, and more. Not that anyone really needs it, but it goes along with the games and guys look forward to it. For some reason, the highly anticipated swag for one Super Bowl . . . never came. Guys were upset. There were a few random T-shirts, but the premium stuff had apparently all been siphoned off by sponsors and business partner guests. The players came last when it came to swag. The people pumping money into marketing coffers got first dibs.

This situation was very disappointing, and the players, coaches, and staff were hurt that sponsors were treated better than members of the team. This could have been an issue, but the team handled it maturely and refused to get distracted. File this situation under "ignore the noise."

I hope by now it is clear what I mean when I say "there's no such thing as the big game." Big moments come down to what you make of them. When you succeed at work, you've created that success. When you win, you've created the win. No win is circumstantial. If you hope to sustain winning, what you are hoping for is to impose your will *on* the circumstances instead of merely waiting for an advantageous moment to appear. If you have a good process, the big games will take care of themselves. As a leader, that means your job is to bring the game back to the basics and not get caught up in the extracurriculars. As a player, that means your job is to perform well under the brightest of lights.

Our process was always the same, every day, whether it was an organized team activity (OTA) day in the spring, the opening game of the season, or a Super Bowl. To win against the best competition, everyone on the team—players, coaches, support people—needed to feel that their job could be the difference in the outcome of the game, so they needed to be performing their job with a minimal amount of distraction and a maximum amount of confidence. My job was to make everyone feel that way. Could Adam Vinatieri's smoking room have made a difference? I don't know, but I do know I don't want to look back at that type of situation with second thoughts.

I know that you will still feel excitement (or dread) about certain momentous occasions in your work—when things can go really well or really badly. What I would ask you to remember is this: *You are one of the reasons the moment is big.* You are not there by accident. Your work brought you to this high-stakes moment. Winning in week four of the regular season isn't the final goal of any player or coach, but my job is to make sure that we all understand that winning in week four *is* part of the process, and gets us prepared to handle bigger challenges.

I've seen veteran players falter under the bright lights despite all their careful preparation, and I've seen rookies succeed. In 2002, we had a quarterback who started the year as the backup, and the Rams had a two-time league MVP (and Super Bowl champion) under center. We won. Six years later *we* were the big favorite in the Super Bowl with many of our players coming in with three rings on their hand—and we were coming off an undefeated season. The Giants were a wild card team that barely made the playoffs and came into the game with little Super Bowl experience. They outplayed us and outcoached us. They won. I'm not saying that every win and loss comes back to how you psychologically manage hoopla, but it makes a difference, and, more important, it's indicative of your overall approach toward winning in general.

You may be a low draft choice, or a cast-off free agent. You were overlooked, doubted, and given up on. Too small, too slow, too old. You may never have competed in the playoffs before. But we brought you here for a reason, and you've proven the naysayers wrong every step of the way. This "big game" is just the next opportunity to do so. If you love football, if you love competition, the stadium will be the place to be regardless of the stakes. That's where you belong.

Cherish being there. My first Super Bowl was in 1987, as defensive coordinator for the New York Giants. We blew the game open in the second half and dominated our way, especially on defense, for the win. After the game, after the on-field jubilation had settled, after the locker room pandemonium, after I'd taken a shower and changed into my regular clothes, after everyone else had filed back out of the locker rooms and onto the buses, I walked out onto the field to have one final look around. It was my first, and there was no guarantee there'd be a second. No more fans, no more players, no more photographers. Just me and some workers cleaning up the Rose Bowl field. And then a security guard came to toss me out. He didn't believe I was a coach. Luckily for me, our linebacker Harry Carson came over and told the guy I was okay, so I got to linger a little longer. You never know how precious—and how rare—those memories are going to be.

THE WORK YOU DID TO GET
TO THE DECISIVE MOMENT IS
THE WORK THAT WILL HELP
YOU CARRY THE DAY. JUST
AS YOU ADAPT TO EVERYDAY
CHALLENGES DURING THE
REGULAR SEASON,
YOU WILL ALSO NEED TO

ADAPT TO THE HEIGHTENED CIRCUMSTANCES IN BIG MOMENTS. SMART PREPARATION AND SMART GAME PLANS GOT YOU THERE; DON'T STOP PREPARING AND GAME PLANNING. AND FINALLY: FILL YOUR DRAWER.

TWO

MOTIVATION

Fans love locker room speeches. They love to see a doughy old coach hop up on a folding chair at halftime and shout nonsense to a group of grown men. Players could be spending that precious time conferring with their teammates or unit coaches about second-half adjustments, or thinking about what they will do when they get back out on the field. And instead the time is spent on someone else trying to make a point. Everyone eats it up. I don't know why.

Imagine your boss sending out a note to employees telling them that they should assemble in the conference room for a special meeting. Imagine him or her stepping up onto the table and shouting about teamwork and togetherness. Maybe you don't have to imagine, because it's happened. (Maybe not the shouting part, but you get the gist.) I have heard and seen in the business world some truly baffling attempts at motivating workforces from above, and

I am here to tell you as a card-carrying member of the coaching world: that is not how motivation works.

I've never been a big team-speech guy. I've never stayed up at night thinking about how to deliver a dramatic pregame speech or banged my head against a locker before charging out onto the field. I do think a leader's *message* to the team is important and can have an impact on the mindset of a team. For the Patriots teams in the 2000s, I found the best way to motivate that group was to convey any disrespect our opponent had shown toward us. Before the 2005 Super Bowl, I became aware of a parade that the city of Philadelphia was already planning if the Eagles won the championship. I shared that information with the team on the morning of the game, with visual aids including a street map of Philadelphia so the guys could visualize the parade. As I was describing the Eagles' victory plans, I could feel the anger building in the room. We were all imagining our opponent holding a parade at our expense.

Did my showing the team a street map of Philadelphia affect the outcome of the game? I don't know, but I do know that the team talked about those parade plans after our victory. It stayed on their minds.

The question I probably get more than any other after any game, win or lose, is "Coach, what did you tell the team at halftime?" I always have one answer, which is that I told them what I tell them every time I stand before them: here are the problems and here's how we fix them.

If you want to go find a smashed chalkboard, go smash one yourself. First, understand that halftime in the locker room is less than ten minutes after accounting for travel time on and off the field. Then it takes a couple minutes for everyone to get organized. So, my first priority in the time remaining is to talk to the coordinators and confirm our second-half planning and adjustments. Those coaching points would then be given to the offense and the defense by the coordinators simultaneously. Finally, I would speak to the team for about two minutes to summarize what we needed to do to win the game. Most of the time, we didn't talk about parade routes.

The concept of "the big speech" implies that someone else's words or actions will, in a single moment, change everything. In my experience, this kind of sudden transformation happens only on rare occasions. The right person, at the right moment, with the right words can trigger the desired response, but in my career these moments have been few and far between. Junior Seau, for instance, was the best pregame speaker I have ever been around. He always had an emotional message that was well-received by the team. In 2007, he kept pushing us all for a perfect season, and we achieved it—in the regular season.

A good speaker can even put a positive spin on a loss. In 2023, after some particularly tough losses, special teams star Matthew Slater often encouraged the team to focus on the positive way they had competed and battled in spite of a general lack of belief in the team from the outside. In the 2017 Super Bowl against the Falcons, the locker room was actually very confident at halftime, despite the Patriots being behind by eighteen points. I told the group that we could only score seven points at a time, and if we focused on each individual play, we could string them together for success. It was just the truth. We could not score eighteen points in one possession, no matter how good a speech I might try to give.

As a leader, it's not about what you need to say. It's about what your team needs to hear. You have to know your players, what they want, what they need, and what drives them. That's why I spend my time thinking about how to *help* the players do their jobs, instead of adding the title "public speaker" to mine.

And that starts with understanding who they are.

· · ·

There's a question that comes up a lot in the player scouting and evaluation process. I doubt that the league would be too excited about it being made public, but I'm going to do it anyway. It's simple but significant: Does the player in question actually *love* football? Taking talent out of the equation, this simple question is probably the most important part of evaluating a player to see if he is a good fit on our teams.

You might be staring at that sentence, mouth open, wondering: *Are there really grown men who put their bodies through hell for years and then sign up for even more years of extremely hard work who don't . . . care about the game?*

Yes.

More than you'd think.

There are players who put everything they have into the game because they can't imagine doing anything else. I'm like that. I don't need coffee; I need more hours in the day. All my energy comes from football—it's endlessly interesting and there's always more to learn and more to do. Whether or not I have a game to prepare for, I work as many hours as when I have film to watch, game plans to devise, and practices to schedule. Why? Because I am still motivated to do the best job I can, which sometimes means explaining the game to television viewers—and, now, to readers. I haven't figured out football and I never will. I accept that. Still, I get up every morning and chase perfection, even though I know it's unattainable.

"Love of the game" players don't need your help to get up for a game. They probably don't need your help to get up for practice. Frankly, as a head coach, I cannot possibly go around and individually motivate seventy players, fifteen coaches, and twenty members of support staff every day. I need to bring in people who *want* to come in and work because they want to be great, and to contribute to a great team.

Love of the game helps especially in those moments when you have to decide whether to make a "business decision" or run into a solid line of bodies in order to make the play, but you'd be surprised how many players, even great players, don't feel the love in that moment. Of course, they probably loved the game to begin with. But eventually they grew weary of the grind, the demands on time, the missed family dinners and holidays—plus the media scrutiny, stress, and extraordinary physical toll the game takes. They have to weigh all that against the reality of retiring and finding a new way to make a living that probably involves getting familiar with signing memorabilia.

Ultimately there is nothing that maximizes talent more than love for the game. An individual's contribution to a win starts with caring more than the other guy.

Let me tell you about someone whose love of the game I actually underestimated—so badly that we almost lost a Super Bowl. Terrell Owens was one of the most talented, dynamic, productive players in the league. A game changer. In December 2004, Owens suffered a severe leg injury and everyone, including the Eagles' medical team, thought he was out for the season. He missed the rest of the regular season and the Eagles' first two playoff games. Our team doctors had relationships with the Eagles' doctors and were told there was no way he could be back for the Super Bowl. When you're a "game plan team," as we always were, you adapt your strategy based on the opponent's most significant threats. So, foolishly working under the assumption that Owens was out, we formulated a game plan, installed it with our players, and practiced for two weeks. And then on the afternoon of February 6, 2005 . . . he was out on the field.

Just a few weeks after breaking his leg and tearing a ligament in his right ankle he decided to "clear himself" and play. That was a big surprise, but we calculated that he wouldn't be operating at full strength, so we kept our game plan to play more man-to-man coverage against the Eagles than had Owens been totally healthy. Over the next three or so hours, Owens shocked everyone: team doctors, the medical community, our players, and certainly me and our coaches. He didn't only play—he played up to his standard. We won the game, but it was *despite* our Terrell Owens miscalculation. He put on a show: nine catches for 122 yards. How did he do it? It started with his love for competing and his love for football. Without those, his physical and mental toughness wouldn't even have been called upon. Not one person thought he could, or should, play, so he had nothing to lose. How many times have we heard about athletes making "business decisions" while staying out of harm's way? Today, we have *perfectly healthy* players managing their workload and opting out of games. Maybe that's a function of today's society and an evolving definition of "love for the game."

But I know that on Super Bowl Sunday in 2005, nobody demonstrated their love for what they do more than Terrell Owens. And it nearly carried the day.

There are players who love the game, and then there are players who are just . . . really good at football. Their talent carries them and helps them succeed. And at a certain point, inertia kicks in. It becomes easier to keep playing the game than quitting. Or they're pushed to continue because of someone else's agenda, or they figure they can make more money playing football than doing almost anything else. But just because they don't love the game like the first category of players doesn't mean they can't still contribute to success.

These players can still be motivated, because motivation can work off selfishness. And that's perfectly okay. We can act like selfishness doesn't exist, like we don't have those kinds of people around us, but we do. There's no reason to be Pollyannaish—to think it's all about the team, that we're one big family, that our people are here just because they want to be with us and would work for free because they love it so much, just isn't how it works. Not in the NFL and not in the real world. (And make no mistake: football might be a game, but it has a way of clarifying some basic truths about the "real world.") There are players whose number one motivator is what's best for them, and them alone, and that's not an automatic turnoff for me, as long as when they play, when they are on the field, they're competing and producing for the betterment of the team. If I can get the best out of a player by meeting him at his most selfish, then I can help that player also put forward the very best advertisement for his skills. For example, if we have a receiver who doesn't want to block, we try to convince him that if he does block, he will benefit on the next play. After blocking the safety on a running play, the receiver will be able to fake a block on an upcoming play and the quarterback will throw him the ball on a play-action pass. The pass simply will not work if he hasn't established that he's a credible blocker—the defense won't react to him. Ultimately, the receiver's self-interest will be satisfied by, first, acting selflessly.

Competition, and work, have a way of transforming selfishness into productivity, and there are a few different ways that we can channel personal incentives into making things happen. First, we identify them. Then, we embrace them.

REPUTATION AS MOTIVATION

Reputation is a funny thing. It's not exactly a virtue like glory or excellence, but it might as well be. In my experience, I've found reputation actually has the ability to cut a lot deeper than both those things. People care about their names. They care about getting the respect they deserve when they work hard. They care about proving people who doubt or demean them wrong. They should. So, before some games, if I felt we were losing steam, I would occasionally veer away from game specifics and tactics and instead find a way to involve the players' reputations in our pregame discussion. Before the biggest games, playoff games, AFC Championship games, I'd go around the room.

"You were supposed to be old, broken-down, and washed-up, Rodney . . ."

"Nobody wanted you, Brady . . ."

"Moss, you're past your prime . . ."

"McCourty, you were supposedly just a special teams player and a reach in the first round . . ."

"David Andrews, you're too small, too unathletic. Nobody wanted you . . ."

I'd be a bit of a jerk about it, up and down the roster, with a personal twist for each guy. I knew it worked on some guys more than others (some guys didn't have much of a reputation to even guard), but our best players always responded—Rodney Harrison, for example, leaned into every slight, real or imagined. But I always ended with: ". . . but this game is why you're here. Not to play the Jets in week two. But for this."

Who knows if they even heard those final words. By then they were all too focused on going out and shutting up the haters. It worked every time.

HONOR AS MOTIVATION

Another approach played to a different set of emotions. Late in my time with the Patriots, we instituted a regular meeting called Play to Honor, which was an opportunity for any player or coach to stand before the team and explain which person in their life they played for—not just the abstract "Why" you'd hear in interviews or articles, but their very real "Who." Over and over, I was blown away by the depth and emotion that many participants showed. Some talked about relatives or friends who had passed away. Others talked about sacrifices that people had made for them throughout their lives so that they could play football for a living: a grandparent who put their life on pause to raise a grandchild, a sibling who struggled with illness but who still found ways to support their brother, or a deceased teammate from a past team. During these full-team sessions, every barrier was broken down. We revealed parts of our lives that we mostly kept private. It wasn't just learning about each other's motivations—*feeling* them all together drew our team closer, made us stronger, and created a common goal: to acknowledge, celebrate, and repay the sacrifice that others had made on our behalf. This was the best way to know your teammates.

Sharing these testimonials worked because it activated a simple principle: You don't let your teammate down. Play for the guy next to you. As much as we all compete with one another at work on the field, everyone should be pulling for each other when the battle is on the line. When you pull together as a team, you also win as a team, and the multiplicative motivational effect becomes a multiplicative *thrill*. No single individual victory feels as good as a team victory. There's infinitely more to honor.

SHAME AS MOTIVATION

I can't talk to everyone in the organization every day. There's just no way I can constantly connect with each player, coach, and staff member to make sure that they are feeling motivated. It's impossible.

That's why to win, and win big, you need motivators *throughout* your organization.

One of mine was New England Hall of Fame linebacker (and excellent coach) Mike Vrabel. Mike was *tough*, a playmaker and culture builder who came through in the clutch during the biggest games. He played several positions and played them all well. He was also highly intelligent, on and off the field, and everything he did was done with purpose and an edginess. Even joking. When he did that, nobody was exempt. Coaches and teammates were both fair game. Mike's knife was always sharp, but it was never malicious—if anything, it made people feel like they were important to the organization if he targeted them. It also helped that he could take it as good as he gave it. If another player responded to his jabs or jokes, they'd be better off, and so would the team.

For years, the Patriots had a vice president of security named Mark Briggs. He was British and a veteran of the British Army—a tough guy, a no-nonsense taskmaster who had seen many things over the course of his career and life and was often around the team. This was before the NFL played games in London, so Mark did not grow up watching the Patriots or following the sport. A player's or coach's status didn't impress him or carry any extra weight when it came to enforcing the team rules. It didn't matter who you were; you followed his rules. But that wasn't the only way Briggs stood out. He also had a prosthetic leg. It didn't seem to affect him at all, even though he constantly had to be up and on the move, making sure that the site was safe and secure.

One day at practice, while the team was in stretching lines, we noticed Briggs running up the access ramps to the middle and upper decks of Gillette Stadium. We often saw him working out at the facility, but on this particular day, it became the focus of attention. One of our young defensive linemen had been out of the lineup for a couple of weeks with what Mike Vrabel deemed to be a minor leg injury. (I qualify "minor" because you never truly know what someone else is feeling, but savvy veterans, and especially ones like Vrabel who have dealt with all kinds of injuries, know which ones need rest and which ones you can play through.) During the stretching session, Vrabel called out the player who was resting, loud enough for everyone to hear.

"See that guy up there?" he said, pointing at Mark. "*He* can run all the way up there and you can't even *practice*?"

Vrabel wasn't afraid to go after coaches too. Once when I announced a weigh-in during a team meeting, he loudly asked me, "Bill, why don't you weigh the coaches? They're all overweight." And couldn't resist continuing the thought with "We have the fattest coaching staff in the league." Talk about reputation.

Now that he's a coach, I wonder what he'd think about getting weighed in.

COLLECTIVE PUNISHMENT

I like to use all the tools in the toolbox. Positive, negative, doesn't matter. If it works, it works. It's all human behavior. And one thing I know about humans is that punishment works.

I can't talk about punishment, though, without talking first about penalties. Penalties are miscues that occur for a variety of reasons, but they all put you at a disadvantage and contribute to losing. When an offensive lineman makes a false start and we move backward five yards, that's not great defense. When we jump offside, that's not the offense doing anything good. It's just a lack of concentration and discipline. If you watch football, you see it every game. Does it make you think, *Just watch the ball*? You and me both. Unintentional penalties are unredeemable. Don't commit them.

If somebody uses AI to summarize this book down to three essential words, I hope they are: Don't. Commit. Penalties.

Over a twenty-year period, we led the league in the fewest personal fouls and fewest pre-snap penalties. Football is a fast game, and some penalties during a play are just going to happen. But penalties before the snap and after the whistle are totally preventable. Coach Parcells would say this to almost every player: "You are not worth penalties." And he'd follow that up with "Belichick, get someone else in there." Or if the penalty was on me as defensive coordinator (e.g., too many men on the field), he would point at me and say, "That includes you too." (He would generally follow that comment up with something inaudible to everyone but me. "Bill, the players love it when I get on your ass!")

Some penalties are impossible to completely eliminate, like in bang-bang situations, when a player moving at full speed arrives a split second early. Others occur when the only way to slow down an elite player on the other team is to hold on a little longer to prevent a catastrophic play. Those kinds of penalties can actually be useful, and tactically advantageous. (Plus, sometimes the refs miss them or let them go, so they're worth the risk—I'll always take a ten-yard offensive holding penalty to prevent our QB from getting blown up and knocked out of the game.) And we teach our defensive backs to grab and tackle the receiver if the receiver beats us in a double move that would result in a touchdown.

Nevertheless, when penalties (either intentional or not) happen in games, the team has to move on immediately to the next play. There is no time for dwelling. But when they happen in practice, there are consequences. It's not five yards. It's laps. For a good part of my career, I'd limit the punishment laps to the player who committed the penalty. He'd make a false start or jump offside, we'd send him off to run his laps, and the next guy would go into the game. Hopefully that would motivate him to improve.

But eventually I figured out a better way to handle it: when one guy jumped, instead of sending him off on his own, the *entire offense* or *entire defense* would have to run. Twenty-five players and another five coaches off doing laps in the middle of practice because of one guy's lack of concentration. It works a lot better than the single-offender approach. You know why? Because as the guilty individual is running, he isn't only thinking about the coach being pissed at him—he's dealing with getting yelled at by everyone else. All those guys who did nothing wrong but still have to run because of him are crushing him every step of the way. His penalty didn't just affect him, so the punishment didn't either. And you better believe that was motivation enough to not make the same mistake twice.

MY MOTIVATION

I am motivated primarily by three things. The first is that I've been to the top, and the top . . . is very good. It could be great to win a golf or tennis tournament, but I can't imagine it being anything like winning a football championship alongside a hundred players, coaches, and staff. You'll never be with a happier group than during a hometown parade or at the banquet when Super Bowl rings are distributed or at a team reunion ten or twenty years later.* I know how deep and powerful of a connection there is between people who have accomplished a rare thing with, and because of, each other. There's only so much room at the top, and I try to get there whenever and however I can.

The second thing that motivates me is simple: I want to be the best. The most effective way I can describe it is a desire to compete all the time, in everything I do. If that brings wins, great. If it doesn't immediately, it will soon.

The fiercest competitors I've been around never stop being competitive, and are authentic and unapologetic in that approach. I enjoyed the great docuseries *The Last Dance*, about Michael Jordan and the dominant Chicago Bulls teams of the 1990s. If you'd ever watched Jordan play basketball, you already knew about his relentless competitiveness. But behind the scenes, you saw that this guy *never* turns it off. He'd go out, score thirty or forty points, win the

---

* I should say, though, that that doesn't mean the people are what make the victory sweet. The victory, on its own, is sweet. Teamwork—and the results you get through it—supersedes bonds of friendship when it comes to winning. You don't have to be best friends with your coworkers, or share your deepest hopes and dreams with them. I've seen people deliriously celebrate a championship together who in any other situation would probably never even talk.

game, and then head back into the locker room and go right into playing a made-up coin toss game with a security guard. It doesn't matter what he's doing—golf, auto racing, baseball, business, whatever. The man lives to compete, and when he competes, he usually wins. (It's why he's apparently worth several billion dollars now, after earning "only" a $100 million salary during his basketball career.) I doubt he had some grand plan about how "if I train myself to try and win when it's not basketball, it will help me win another championship." It's not intentional. It's innate.

And here's a secret: competition *is* fun. If you can develop a way to constantly want to compete, you'll start seeing situations at work and in life that can be turned into a game. Games are fun, especially when you win. Even if you're the only one playing, you can still keep score. I often made up my own games as head coach. For instance, if the media clearly wanted me to say something, I tried hard not to.

The third thing that motivates me is less fun, but no less important: fear of failure. Because I love winning, the feeling I have after losing a game is brutal, and significantly more intense than the elation I feel holding a trophy. After a loss, it's critical to remember that feeling of disappointment. But that's not fear of failure. Fear is not disappointment. Disappointment sucks you inward and it keeps you from moving forward. Real fear makes you run toward something. I am afraid of losing, so I am constantly trying to move forward with my eyes open, toward the win.

Mark Bavaro, a legendary New York Giant of the 1980s, was one of the greatest players I ever coached. Mark and Rob Gronkowski were the best tight ends I coached, and I had the privilege of coaching a lot of good ones. Regardless of position, Mark would absolutely be in the running for toughest football player ever. In all my years of coaching, the most competitive drills I saw were the NY Giants outside linebackers versus the tight ends—that meant Mark

Bavaro taking on Carl Banks and Lawrence Taylor, day after day. Theirs was a respectful battle that made all three players better. All three would tell you that those practices were tougher than almost any game, and the tight ends coach, Mike Pope, and I learned so much from watching those three greats compete.

One time, during a game, Bavaro had a nasty collision with a defensive player and went in for an X-ray, which revealed a broken jaw. He not only returned to the game but showed up to practice the next day, with his jaw wired shut, and proceeded to play that way for weeks. It was incredible. It's not that Mark was fearless (irrational fearlessness in the NFL would quicky get you put on the injured reserve list), but he was conditioned by his competition in practice to not want to lose, ever. His elite teammates made him hate losing. That's one reason that real toughness will never come with a perfect winning record, because real toughness seeks out the best competition.

All these motivators come from different places, but they have one important thing in common: they keep us moving. As a leader, part of your job is learning about your team and determining what will work best for different people. As an individual, part of your job is not waiting around for a leader to unlock your motivation, but finding a way—through shame, honor, fear, or the sheer desire to participate in the euphoria of the winning moment—to get yourself on track, working at least as hard as the man with one leg.

DON'T WAIT AROUND
EXPECTING SOMEONE ELSE
TO MOTIVATE YOU.
IF COMPETITION ITSELF
DOESN'T GET YOU GOING,
EMBRACE JEALOUSY.
ACCEPT A CERTAIN AMOUNT
OF SELFISHNESS AS LONG
AS SELFISHNESS CAN BE
CHANNELED TOWARD WINNING
HABITS. LET YOURSELF

BE ASHAMED OF BAD PERFORMANCES. ONCE YOU GET EVERYTHING YOU CAN OUT OF SELFISHNESS, FINISH THE JOB BY FIGHTING FOR THE PERSON NEXT TO YOU. THEY'LL BE DOING THE SAME. FINALLY, IF YOU ARE AS LUCKY AS ME, YOU WILL LOVE WHAT YOU DO FOR WORK, AND NOTHING CAN TOUCH THAT MOTIVATION.

THREE

FIRING AND HIRING

There was not much love in the air in Cleveland on Valentine's Day 1996. The season was over, one of the most loyal and passionate fan bases in all of sports was left in the cold, feeling outraged and betrayed, and I was out of a job. (I could write a book on the whole Cleveland experience. It would . . . not be a book about winning.)

Here's what happened: in the middle of our season—on November 6, 1995—Art Modell, the owner of the Browns at the time, announced a deal, pending final approval by the NFL, that would relocate the team to the city of Baltimore, Maryland. A sports team relocation is a firing on a mass scale, and the carnage to careers and livelihoods can reverberate for years. Very few people know what it's like to be in charge of a football team and have the entire season overshadowed—and scuttled—by something that has nothing to do with football. (But then again, plenty of people have experience with bosses whose interests are not necessarily aligned with the interests of his or her employees. And many more of you surely have experience with a boss who says one thing in, say, November, but then says something very different in February. A boss whose relationship with honesty is seemingly . . . ambivalent.)

Despite the massive upheaval, Modell assured me for the subsequent three months that I would remain head coach and move to Baltimore along with the franchise when the time came. It put me in a strange position, but a relatively secure one. We kept it together. We kept playing football.

Moving a team in the middle of the season was unprecedented, and for good reason. While Modell was holding parades in Baltimore, his team was back in Cleveland. When the conquistador Hernán Cortés landed his soldiers in Mexico from Spain, he ordered the ships that had conveyed them to be burned, to eliminate any chance of retreat. It seemed to me that Modell "burned the boats" too, and left his team with little hope for the future.

As chaotic as things were inside the team building in Berea, Ohio, everything outside the walls was worse. Fans were up in arms and out in the streets, picketing team headquarters, protesting, and generally mourning the impending loss of their beloved team; I watched them disassemble rows of seats and throw them off the upper deck of the old Cleveland Municipal Stadium in the Browns' final home game against the Bengals. The Cleveland fans were so violent in the second half that the teams had to switch directions on the field to avoid getting too close to the Dawg Pound section of the stands, where fans were hurling objects onto the field. It was anarchy, but hardly surprising in retrospect. Announcing a relocation months in advance of actually relocating, with games still left to play, was a wholly predictable formula for insanity. It was like telling your girlfriend you plan to break up with her in three months. So let's have fun until then!

It didn't help matters that two years prior I had released the local-legend quarterback Bernie Kosar. I'd had plenty of experience with firing people by that point, but experience does not necessarily equate to effectiveness.

I was about six inches shorter than Kosar, and about 100 percent less beloved in Cleveland. He had been the local hero for years, born in Youngstown, near where my own family hailed from. He spent three years at the University of Miami for college, won them a national championship, and then made it to the NFL in 1985, when he was drafted by the Browns in the supplemental draft. Halfway through his first season, he took over for the starting QB, who had sustained an injury, and never looked back. For the next four seasons he took the team and the city to new heights of success, including three AFC Championship games. He didn't win a Super Bowl, but he won Clevelanders' respect and adoration. To them, he was one of their own: a tough blue-collar worker who stood up and performed when he was called on.

Unfortunately, though, time comes for us all. Especially in football. By the early nineties, Bernie had suffered two tough injuries, one to his throwing arm and one to his ankle. He was one of the toughest players I ever coached, but at a certain point he was simply unable to overcome those two injuries and return to his late-eighties form. Our own relationship had also soured—after a game in November 1993, he'd boasted to the press about how he had drawn up a touchdown play all on his own, i.e., without the wrong-headed meddling of Coach Belichick. (We'll talk about good ways of firing people, but I would suggest that a good way to *get* fired is to shout to the media that you're smarter than your boss.) As a staff, we collectively agreed that it was best to release Bernie, and I made my recommendation to Modell. Bernie Kosar was released on November 8, 1993.

That should have been the whole story. I should have been able to explain to all the parties involved that we needed better play at the quarterback position, and that the best chance for us to win would be to start someone else. It was the right thing to do. It was *not* the right way to do it. My mismanagement of the situation didn't help matters. And it didn't help my career. I should have been prepared to honor and respect the public adoration that existed for Kosar, and to anticipate the psychological implications of that adoration for Kosar himself. I have no doubt that the seeming suddenness of the decision, paired with my somewhat clinical explanation of Kosar's decline at the press conference announcing his release, inflamed an already difficult situation within the locker room and more generally in and around Cleveland.

When Modell announced the Cleveland-to-Baltimore move, the fans were mad at me, at Art Modell, at the NFL. They were mad, period. This was when I first learned about the importance of blocking out the noise and only focusing on what you can control. I thought it would be possible to put my head down and move forward because Modell had told me the job was still mine. He wasn't firing *me*. I wasn't so naive to think I would be in Baltimore for a long time, but at least in the meantime I was safe. So when Modell changed his mind and did fire me, I felt lied to, misled, and wronged. I'm sure you have too, whether you've been fired or merely been reprimanded for things that are outside of your control.

I'm not saying this to garner sympathy. That's sports. Winning makes people happy and losing makes people mad. Losing games is one thing; losing your entire team, as the Cleveland fans did, is something entirely different. So when I got fired, a lot of those fans were happy. Even though they already knew the team was leaving, they were happy to see me left behind on the way out. Finally I was just like everyone else. Because *everyone* has been fired. Everyone has been blamed, scapegoated, and sacrificed. Now I knew what it felt like, right?

The Browns packed up and moved out. They won a Super Bowl, as the Ravens, a few years later in 2001, and then again in 2013. In the final analysis, Modell's initial $4 million investment in the Browns turned into a franchise worth several hundred million dollars thirty-five years later. Unfortunately, Modell was several million dollars in debt. Modell initially sold some of the team (and eventually all of the team) to Steve Bisciotti. Now Baltimore has one of the best owners in the NFL, a stable and consistent franchise, and a great fan base. The "new" Browns (Modell was not able to take the name to Baltimore) were purchased by Jimmy Haslam and "returned" to Cleveland in 1999 as an expansion team. Since then the Browns have won one playoff game, in 2021, and had thirty-eight (and counting) starting quarterbacks and multiple changes in their coaching staff and front office. Steve Bisciotti is a prime example of what good ownership can do for a franchise. He established stability in the front office with executive vice president of player personnel Ozzie Newsome and head coach John Harbaugh. And the Ravens have been very competitive for twenty-plus years and counting.

For those reasons and more, I believe that what happened in Cleveland was catastrophically bad management and a textbook case in how not to end things. Not only did the process enrage much of the city, it also drained the confidence many people had in anything the owner might say about the future of the team. I use the story as an illustration of just how an organization can go sideways.

Firing someone should be done humanely, compassionately, and honestly because that's the right thing to do, period, but also, it signals to the rest of the organization that *this is how we do things.*

I know that because I was fired, badly.

But I also know it because I, too, have fired, badly.

This is a chapter about endings and beginnings, and how to win through both.

At my very first job, with the Baltimore Colts in 1975, our training camp was at Goucher College in Towson, Maryland. Camps in those days were a grueling eight-week march. There was the training, of course—day in, day out. But there was also the knowledge that, after all of it, not everyone would make the team. Most guys usually had a decent feel for whether they'd be kept or cut by the end. They could do the math. Still, the anticipation and the uncertainty were stressful—and things got harder when players expected to make the final roster but didn't.

When you're the new guy, or "new dude," as the role is universally called in pro sports circles, you get all the jobs nobody else wants. Some new dudes see it as a curse. I always thought of it as a blessing. The better you do in those roles, the more confident your superiors are in giving you more. The more you get to do, the more you learn and the more valuable you become. Some new dudes don't see it that way and they become old dudes pretty fast. They like doing what they like and that's it. They don't last.

Which is how I ended up with the unenviable task of going door-to-door through the Goucher College dorms to inform each player being cut that they had to go see the head coach and general manager. It wasn't my job to tell them why, but they knew what the knock on the door meant.

A new nickname, "Bad News Billy," was born.

Once the players saw me, they knew why I had come. It was tough on them. And, honestly, it was tough on me too. When you're twenty-four and younger than practically every player you're about to usher to their release, it's not easy. On top of that, I was *significantly* shorter and smaller than men who were about to enter the real world to go find real jobs. I knew if any one of those players wanted to take his frustrations out on me, it would be over quickly—goodbye, Bad News Billy.

I'm not going to try to be some new age life coach about this. Losing isn't winning. Failures aren't successes. Getting fired isn't a gift. Getting fired is tough. It's traumatic. I don't use that word lightly, but it is. During normal times, it's easy enough to imagine that your job and your life are two distinct domains—family is family, and work is work. But when you get fired, that distinction gets bulldozed. You have bills to pay, childcare to arrange, food to put on the table. All the basics and necessities of providing for a family and contributing to the future are suddenly less secure. It's very personal indeed.

To be the person who brings all that, literally, to someone's door is not ideal. But sometimes it has to be done.

The key is how you do it.

After Cleveland, I rejoined my old boss Bill Parcells in New England. He taught me that players lose their starting job, or are replaced or fired, for one of two reasons: "Either you aren't playing well or someone is playing better." That's it. Someone else can do it better, and that someone else is in the building.

That's why I had made the determination to release Bernie Kosar. We had someone who could do the job better—Vinny Testaverde, who would go on to be an NFL starter for another decade. In my experience, being fired usually has nothing to do with politics or favoritism or anything subjective at all. It has to do with cold,

LAWRENCE TAYLOR

Lawrence Taylor wore number 56 during his career. So page 56 is reserved for him.

In my opinion, LT was the greatest defensive player to ever play the game. He came into the league in 1981 as an elite talent and was the Defensive Rookie of the Year. He had a remarkable level of physical and mental toughness. Taylor was the ultimate competitor, and would compete at everything.

George Rogers was the number one pick in the 1981 draft. LT was number two. I liked to remind LT about Rogers being the first pick. George never did much against us. LT made sure of that.

LT was the cornerstone of some great Giants' linebacker groups that I had the honor to coach. He was the Defensive Player of the Year three times and the league MVP once. He tilted the field. Opposing offenses had to always pay attention to him, and he understood how to use that attention to help his teammates be more productive. And I can't count the number of times LT should have dropped into coverage, but he blitzed and sacked the QB.

I admit that I was annoyed a few times when LT dozed off in meetings. But I couldn't get too upset. When I handed out the linebacker test on Friday morning, he was always the first one finished and usually had the fewest mistakes. His football instincts were off the charts—he knew his assignments, and surprisingly, he knew what everyone else on the defense did.

LT would have had a great career without me, but I don't know where I would be without him. I am forever indebted to LT and to Coach Parcells for allowing me to coach the best defensive player ever.

Taylor deserved great coaching. I tried to give him my best.

hard calculations. The beauty of accepting this is that it means you do not have to take it personally. It is mechanical: This unit is superior to that unit. Swap them.

I've never stopped being Bad News Billy. From Towson, Maryland, to Cleveland to New England, I've had to release hundreds of players and make countless staff decisions. I've fired a lot of people. But I believe that if you talked to the players I've released, they would tell you that, even if they disagreed with my decision, I did it with respect. (In some cases, they might actually admit that everything all worked out for the best.) Some people are woken up by being let go, and begin to self-assess—partly out of necessity, but partly out of a new, hard-won commitment to doing what it takes to last wherever they go next.

My commitment to firing people with dignity comes in part because I've been fired myself—both as an assistant coach and as a head coach. Almost every coach has been. And I've seen how when a whole coaching staff gets fired, the situation is toughest on the assistants. The head coach is in a better position financially and professionally to take care of himself and land on his feet. The assistant coaches, meanwhile, are scrambling, and the coach they've been working for is now out of a job. When I left an organization as the head coach, I tried to help the people who were loyal to me. That was difficult because in both cases, I didn't immediately move into a new head coaching position. I wanted to help them as much as possible, but I simply did not have the opportunity to do so. When you are the person being let go, the first thing I recommend is to recalibrate: Figure out what you want to do, even if that opportunity is not available. Then consider what will put you in the best position to get what you want in the next hiring cycle. I can sum this up in three words: Have a plan!

The chief error of the Browns firing in 1995, in my opinion, was not the decision. It was the execution. The "plan," such as it existed, did not take human nature—or humans, period—into account. It seemed to flow mostly from purely logistical and financial considerations. That's fine if you're leaving your city anyway and burning every bridge, but if you're going to still be part of the equation, I highly recommend stage-managing this emotional part of business to an extreme degree. The responsibility is on you to help the person getting fired understand the mechanical nature of the decision. You need to be prepared to fire people as you're prepared to do every other part of your job. No amount of compassion and humanity will outweigh the hurt of a bad plan. If you fire badly, you leave behind a mess, look like an amateur, and send a signal to the rest of your team that you aren't in control and don't have their best interests in mind.

I'll give you an example of "firing without a good plan": my worst roster cutdown ever.

The few days around the roster cutdown period constitutes probably the busiest stretch of an NFL season. Especially when the organizational structure is such that the head coach is also responsible for personnel decisions, as I was in New England.

Each year, in the span of forty-eight hours in late August or early September, I would do a deep dive into team preparation. I would make a final assessment of the roster. I would make a projection of the timetable for the return of players who were already injured or coming back from medical treatments over the offseason. I would consider trade options. I would look at financials. I would release dozens of players and re-sign another dozen to our practice squad. I would pore through the list of twelve hundred players who had just been released by the other thirty-one teams and look for any opportunities there. Simultaneously, the coaching staff would be preparing for the opening game and getting into the regular-season routine.

A few hours before the NFL-mandated four o'clock roster reduction deadline, we made our decisions and were ready to meet with each player, in person. We were able to catch some of the guys before they headed out to the party, but one of the soon-to-be-released players was already there, ninety minutes away from the office—literally, at that moment, in the pool with his family. A member of our staff was cast in the role of Bad News Billy and had to inform the player that he needed to see the head coach. *While he was still in the pool.* It was the worst handling of a roster move I have ever been a part of. Embarrassing for the player, his family, his teammates; for me; and for our whole program.

I vowed to never be caught without a plan for cutdown again. I made releasing players with dignity the highest priority, and from that day forward, every player release was handled with appropriate measures. Never, ever again would I allow the avalanche of decisions and meetings that surround cutdown day to compromise what every player deserves: respect. That includes a conversation with the chief decision-maker—me—and an opportunity to have a dialogue about what went into the decision and advice on how to move forward. There was a new standard: anything but what happened that day on Cape Cod.

Former CEO of General Electric Jack Welch gave me some good advice in my early years in Foxborough. "Treat your employees with the same love and respect on the way out the door as you do on the way into the organization." I have always tried to respectfully talk to every person who I did not retain. I almost always broke the news in person, and tried to get the termination handled before it was released to the public. This wasn't always possible—sometimes I had to release a player over the phone or notify their agent if I couldn't reach the player. Some organizations release players by slipping a note under the door in the middle of the night, telling the player to pack his bags and be ready to turn in his playbook so he can get to the airport at 7 a.m. Talk about a wake-up call.

An employee who was fired will remember the process and the way he was treated. He will tell his remaining friends on the team about the experience. For everyone's benefit, follow Welch's advice and treat employees the same on the way in as you do on the way out (unless they have done something egregious). Most of us have been on both sides of this difficult conversation.

Before determining the specific composition of any team you are coaching, you must identify what you are looking for in every major group of the team, and how all the major groups fit together. These groups would include: coaching staff, offensive line, scouting department, and medical department. You should have a vision of how you want the team to look on the football field, how you want them to compete in the most intense games, and how to select, teach, and train the team to behave during those games. Do you want your team to be quick, fast, tough, highly conditioned, smart, and disciplined? The answer to all of those questions is, of course, yes. But you will have to prioritize—if you want a fast team, you get fast players, but you may have to give up some attributes in other areas (for example: size, intelligence, toughness). Do you want an experienced coach—or do you want a super high-energy coach at a certain position? Have a good plan, stick to the plan the best you can, and be ready to adjust (and improve) constantly as you go forward. The NFL season is long, and you must consider the growth and improvement of the team (as well as the possible decline from aging or potentially injured players). You cannot expect that all your changes will work perfectly—expect to keep fine-tuning your team every hiring cycle.

Once the team is selected, the most important job for the head coach is to evaluate how each group and individual is performing. The evaluation should be comprehensive to include each player, coach, and support person—identify what they are good at, what they bring to the team, and what they need to change or improve. Communicate your evaluation to each employee. After the 2002 Super Bowl, I sat with the coaching and personnel staff and listed twenty-six players who needed to be upgraded for us to have a championship roster. We had just won a championship, and we identified half our team as needing to improve or be replaced. That meeting was an eye-opener for some in the room, but to me, it showed that our staff was committed to building a winning team and not satisfied with riding in a parade. If we hadn't improved on that team, we would not have had any more parades.

In football, players and coaches move around to different teams all the time. There's a lot of beginnings and endings, even before any of our careers are done. We're used to starting over. Having the opportunity to do so isn't always a bad thing, but it's not easy either. Although not a traumatic change, like getting fired is, joining a new company can be highly stressful and involve learning about new ways of doing business, new social expectations, and new people. There are ways, though, to approach it and maximize your chances of thriving.

Yes, the most important thing is to always Do Your Job, but every workplace is about more than results. It's about people. It's about culture. If your workplace is thriving and racking up wins, emulate that. Extend it. Lift it up and live by it. If everyone is stuck in the mud, look around, observe, and understand why, so that when the time comes, you can change it.

On day one, the most important thing to do is to get an accurate read of the room. What's the environment you're entering? Who are you replacing? What mistakes did they make? Most critically: Who in the organization is untouchable? What influence do they have, why do they have it, and what did they do to earn it? And just as important: What do your colleagues want from you? Is it what *you* want?

There's a scene in *The Godfather* in which Michael Corleone is preparing for a meeting to straighten out the differences between the rival mob families, and his father, Vito, gives him some advice: "Whoever proposes that meeting would be the traitor." And, sure enough, Salvatore Tessio, one of the don's oldest associates and friends, is the one who speaks to Michael about arranging the sit-down . . . and then must pay the ultimate price for his betrayal. The lesson is clear. Sometimes when you start a new position, the people who voluntarily insert themselves into your life are the ones who are working their own agenda. I hope you are not involved in organized crime. Either way, there's much to learn from the old man's warning.

I'm willing to bet that, when you start somewhere new, a couple of people at least—usually well entrenched in the organization, well-liked, mid-to-senior management—will go out of their way to welcome you on day one. They'll offer up a friendly, servant attitude and pledge to help you with "whatever you need."

At first this'll sound great. You've got allies! Already! And who doesn't want allies? But I encourage you to think more deeply about why they're standing in front of your desk. I'm not saying they're plotting to sell you out to a competitor like Tessio—you're the new guy, and you don't have much power at all yet—but I've found that these "whatever you need" people are the ones to be leeriest of when you start a new job. Sure, they might help out from time to time, but only under certain conditions, spoken or unspoken. Take note of the circumstances when they offer and try to understand their motives.

They might use the difference in experience, status, or tenure to arbitrarily and self-servingly lay down expectations for your job, when those are not the things you were hired to handle. They might be willing to help out, but only if their help is delivered in such a way that other people—the real decision-makers—are around to see it. Remember that help offered only in public is help with an asterisk, and then go ahead and make use of it. If they want to use you, use them back. Just don't fall for their game, and don't permit them to treat you like an underling forever. They will try. And then lay low and wait until they're back in their cubicles so you can put your head down and get to work. You will be noticed—if not by the powers that be at your current workplace, then by their competitors.

Remember what Parcells said about being replaced: "Either you aren't playing well or someone is playing better." Wise words to help you get over the personal shock of being fired, but also wise words to help ward off complacency. Never stop watching. Never stop being afraid. There will always be someone better. If someone better doesn't exist yet, become that person.

And then take the job.

Once you do, you'll inevitably find yourself on the other side of the dreaded interview desk. It will be your turn to ask the questions and to take the measure of someone you've just met. It's not easy, and it shouldn't be. Too much is at stake. We're talking about human beings and livelihoods, and we're talking about winning. It takes careful work and concentration to think through the composition of a workforce, and to try to spot talent among the sea of mediocrity.

I loved hiring young people. Some of the golden eras of my career were when I was hiring our first generations of entry-level coaches and scouts in New England and in Cleveland. One group of these young coaches was affectionately called the 20/20 Club on the basis that they tended to work twenty hours a day for about $20,000 per year. They were fresh. They were clear. They knew the stakes, and the opportunity: if we hired them, they would have a chance to make their name (and ours). None of them had an agenda that they were secretly polishing and implementing in order to prove they knew better; they knew they were entering an established framework—mine. They all had something bigger to prove. When I considered new hires, I tried to discern three fundamental things: Do you love football? Do you work hard? Are you intelligent? If the answers were yes, yes, and yes, we were good to go. Their skills and our system were a perfect combination. Because we had established in New England such a culture of accountability (from the beginning, I'd made clear that I was willing to bench or cut veteran talent if they stopped helping us win), we were happy to spread our trust around to anyone who made it past our rigorous screening. That trust earned loyalty.

Hiring, though, is more than loyalty and willingness to be part of a system. It's about a drive to win. Our process of vetting candidates for coaching jobs often involved days of meetings, film sessions, and elaborate tests, during which we asked candidates to watch film on college players and free agents and offer their evaluations. We weren't just trying to gauge their physical and mental stamina (those meetings can be taxing to the point of physical exhaustion); we were weeding out the coaches and scouts who loved the game from those who were simply talented observers of it. Talent at this level is a given. But talent can coast. Talent alone doesn't sleep on the office couch so there's no wasted time in the morning before watching more film. Talent doesn't volunteer to catch balls from a fifth-string QB who wants a few more reps in September to try out some new footwork. Talent complains about hotel accommodations. Talent thinks they know better. People who love the game just want to win the game. And they will, no matter what it takes. They know their essential value is being part of an overall unit and being someone who can put work into any system. (I'm a big fan of this kind of thinking, if I haven't made that clear.)

Hiring this way has produced results—not just wins, but a steady progression of high-standard operating. When you teach someone from the ground up how to work a system, they help the system stay focused and intact. This creates perspective and keeps people invested, and when we hire again, everyone expects a sustained level of success. Another method we implemented in our vetting process was weighing some votes more heavily than others—primarily those of the guys who used to have the job the new guy was interviewing for. They knew what that job needed more than anyone else, even me. I always put the onus on coaches who were being elevated. I'd tell them: "You've earned additional responsibility and a new position for yourself, but the next guy better not break the chain. If you recommend someone and he can't do the job, you'll not only have your new responsibilities, you'll get your old ones back too."

The best example of this working out was when I hired Brian Daboll based on the strong recommendation of Nick Saban. Daboll was at Michigan State and he mailed examples of his work to my home. His work was impressive, but as I learned when I was young, getting a job is more about who you know than what you know. Which is to say: Nick Saban's recommendation carried a lot more weight than any portfolio. Daboll proceeded to do a great job for me as a quality-control defensive coach. By November of 2000, our first year, it was clear to me that Daboll would become a great coach for us and I wanted to promote him, but I couldn't because he was too valuable in his quality-control role. When he understandably asked about a promotion, I told him that he had to stay in his job until he found and trained someone to replace him. Well, Daboll went and did it, so he could move up the ranks. The man who he had found to replace him at QC? Josh McDaniels. Josh and Brian were two future head coaches with a passion for football and an elite work ethic. This process did not end there. When it was Josh's turn to get promoted, he hired Nick Caserio, the future general manager of the Houston Texans, as his replacement.

Remember when I said that my strategy for winning football games is to score more points than the other team? I have a similar strategy for hiring and firing: hire good people and fire people who aren't that good (with respect and dignity). If you're able to execute on both those rules, you'll do well. I hope I've made it clear in this chapter, though, that there are other factors at play when we make changes to our workforces. The hiring process, on both sides of the exchange, can be a way to strengthen and recommit to the fundamental principles of any organization. And likewise for when it's time to fire someone: do it in a way that sends a message to the rest of your organization about what you stand for, what level of excellence you expect—and how decently you will treat people on the way out. Never waste an opportunity to make sure your team knows that you see them as human beings. Winning requires hard choices, but hard choices do not require cruelty.

Of all the staff people I hired, I think my best move was hiring Ernie Adams. I met Ernie at Phillips Academy—he was a senior and I was a postgraduate. Ernie played guard and I played center. We became good friends and shared a common interest in football, and more specifically in coaching. Ernie was instrumental in helping me get hired as the special teams coach under Ray Perkins at the New York Giants. Ernie and I worked together in three organizations, and he was my right-hand man on every major decision. Ernie was a voice of moderation and analysis—he gave me unbiased opinions that helped me do my job. In the 2002 draft, we had the 253rd selection and the board was picked clean. There weren't any players left who we thought would make our roster. I turned to Ernie and asked him to find somebody. He came up with wide receiver David Givens—good pick!

RESPECT THE PEOPLE OF CLEVELAND. TREAT PEOPLE WITH KINDNESS, RESPECT, AND DIGNITY WHENEVER YOU ARE MAKING A DECISION THAT INVOLVES THEIR LIFE OUTSIDE OF WORK. DON'T LET YOURSELF GET SUCKED INTO BAD WORKPLACE CULTURE AS A NEW HIRE.

WORKFORCES WITH A MIXTURE OF EXPERIENCE AND HUNGER CAN COMBINE VERY EFFECTIVELY. WHEN AN EMPLOYEE WANTS A PROMOTION, DON'T PROMOTE THEM UNTIL THEY HAVE TRAINED THEIR REPLACEMENT. AND, SERIOUSLY, RESPECT THE PEOPLE OF CLEVELAND.

FOUR

HANDLING SUCCESS

S o, it all went better than you expected. The client just sent a happy email and signed up for another round. The numbers looked even better than you were hoping for. The funding came in. You're finally going to get the recognition you deserve. But there's something bugging you when you get home. *This is all temporary*, the voice in your head says. Who knows if your boss will even remember this at the end of the year when compensation gets reviewed. Nothing is a sure thing. Part of you knows that you got lucky this time. You worked hard, sure, but you only played a small part in a larger outcome.

How do you fight back against this feeling?

You don't. Your feeling is accurate. One good outcome doesn't mean anything. It could have been a fluke—they do happen. In the NFL, any team might leap up from the bottom of the standings to the playoffs the next season. (They call it "parity" if they're being polite.) You could call it random, and you wouldn't be wrong. But do you want to randomly succeed? Or do you want to actively win?

Success comes in different shapes and sizes. Immediate success, like when a pass rusher defeats a blocker and sacks the quarterback, or when someone scores a touchdown on a big play, is great for the player and the team. But those successes are momentary, and other than padding personal stat lines, there's more to do to really win.

Then there's long-term success, the kind that you and I are trying to nail down in this book. The kind of success that contains moments but does not start and stop with each game result, or quarterly earnings.

If you're reading this book, you've had your share of moments. They probably made you hungry for more, and you feel like you're not getting fed enough. The problem might be your relationship to your success. Are you too proud of what you've done? Or even worse, are you confusing what you've *actually* done with things that merely happened *around* you and *to* you? As Shakespeare said: "Some are born great, some achieve greatness, and some have greatness thrust upon them." The only one that matters is the middle. No one is born great in this country, and it doesn't matter if you stumble into greatness—you'll stumble out of it.

You have to ask yourself what you really want. Are you good with having your one moment? You're going to have to decide that for yourself, because that's the essence of success. Is it worth the trouble? You know my answer.

The only success that matters is sustained success. Success that lasts longer than a mere interval in between other, equivalently likely outcomes. That's when it's apparent that there's an author— or artist—behind the W and not just another guy who got his number called. Success is not a solid, straight line. It might seem that way, but below the surface there is plenty going on to keep things level. There is no way for it to work otherwise. Not in life, and not in football. Not over the course of an entire season, and definitely not over the course of seasons and decades.

There was a stretch of years where the Patriots brand may have been viewed that way—one long, easy, continuous, unthreatened victory. But day to day and year to year, we were constantly self-assessing and going through restarts. As Tedy Bruschi said during a winning streak in 2003 and 2004, we didn't win twenty-one games in a row; we won one game twenty-one times. Understand this difference. Each game was its own battle.

In this chapter I'm going to illustrate what I think the difference is between handling success, which sets you up for more to come, and merely coasting with the misplaced faith that winning sustains itself in some kind of magical act of physics. It won't. Not without more work, more adaptation, and more preparation.

This book is about sustained high performance and winning, so, naturally, it will feature a lot of stories about Tom Brady. He handled success by using it to fuel his drive for more, and the result was not a straight line but a vector that pointed upward until it ended past the point of all measurement. In the best way, he made a mockery of a league more or less built to give every team the same likelihood of winning.

But one of the great things about sports is the debates and comparisons. ("My guy's better! You can't compare eras! Look at his supporting cast vs. his!") I've never engaged in this argument with my good friend Andy Reid, the Kansas City Chiefs' head coach, but I have little doubt he will write his own book one day and claim that *he* had the greatest QB of all time. You know what? Brady and Patrick Mahomes are both really good. Controversial, I know.

That's a battle for another day, but now that Tom is retired, I think it's safe to talk for a minute about why Patrick Mahomes has been on top and probably isn't going anywhere. His success reminds me a lot of the guy I coached, the guy who obliterated any impediment to winning, again and again, over weeks, months, years, and decades.

And it has everything to do with how they both handle success.

One example sticks out to me. Early in the 2024 season, the Kansas City Chiefs had just come away with a narrow Sunday Night Football win in Atlanta, improving their record to a perfect 3–0. Mahomes was interviewed after the game. What was the vibe? *Chiefs win again, rinse, repeat, let's hear from the three-time Super Bowl Most Valuable Player, two-time league Most Valuable Player.* You can probably imagine the scene. A team in the middle of a historic dynasty, off to another great start, in pursuit week by week of records and accomplishments that few other teams have ever sniffed. And on top of it all, a bona fide superstar on and off the field. Almost anyone in his position would have taken the opportunity to advertise his obvious greatness.

What did we get from Mahomes?

"I feel like I haven't played very well, and that's not a stats thing. I just feel like I'm missing opportunities whenever they're out there and not throwing the ball in the exact spot I want it to be at."

This kind of comment is music to my ears. Can't get enough of it. I want to make that sound bite my cell phone ringtone. It is fundamentally an example of elite leadership. Very similar to when we would win a game with Tom 28–10 and afterward he'd say, "We should have scored forty-five!"

But should we really be surprised? Mahomes is not just someone who's happy to be there, some dude who just banked a W and now thinks he's got it all figured out. This is *Patrick Mahomes.* You think three wins in September does it for him? Think starting an NBA season 9–1 had Michael Jordan feeling great? No way. By putting himself on the spot, by publicly doubting the basis for the W that he just secured, Mahomes sent a powerful message to, and about, his entire team: *This may look okay right now, but it's not going to be good enough in the end.* And that says to me that the Chiefs aren't going anywhere as long as number 15 is on the field. Were they winning? Sure. But they were also not playing up to their highest standard. Mahomes recognized it, and then promised more. *We didn't win the way we need to win. But we will.*

Maybe that's not the cool thing to do. I'm sure there were rookies and new players in the Chiefs locker room who were just ecstatic to win another game and weren't thinking immediately about what else could be done. (Good for them.) Some were likely caught off guard by their leader's comments, and thought he needed to lighten up. *Why is he always so hard on everyone?* they might have thought as he walked by. They didn't understand then, but I guarantee you they'll understand eventually. Or they'll be on someone else's team. People like Tom and Patrick have a way of surrounding themselves with other guys who get the picture—and shaking off the guys who don't.

Both Tom and Patrick understand that the mistakes you made while squeaking out a W are not washed away by a final score. You can look the other way and think those things won't bring you down, but while you're doing that, they'll fester and grow, and then they eventually will bring you down, when you least expect it. Patrick Mahomes, Tom Brady, and everyone who buys into their methods knows this, and it's why they sometimes come off in public as frustrated or even joyless. It's because they don't wait for a real crisis to fix things. They don't wait until the last moment to prepare and then feel proud if they miraculously stick the landing. They proactively set out to *prevent* crises.

Sometimes you succeed despite your flaws. It's okay to be fortunate in that way. You got away with it, for now, and you know it. But you need to take that success and immediately put it behind you. Ignore it. Focus only on the incompleteness of the win. Handle your success by actually analyzing what you did that led to it, and what you failed to do to make the win more convincing.

I always thought that several annual review periods were important, regardless of your position or title. After each offseason program, draft, training camp, game, and season, I would look back at our results, good and bad. Some organizations have quarterly reports—in football, the cycle is defined by the focus of each period: team selection, training, and competition. Everything matters. So I would use the reviews to make everything in our organization be done at a championship level. I would ask everyone to check their ego at the door and be honest in evaluating the job we did in the selected time frame. Basically, three questions had to be answered: What did we do well? What needs to be improved? What would we do differently the next time? This type of honest analysis led to improvements throughout our process, including for myself. I continued to learn how the team and I could do things better in our next cycle.

The truth about any one success is that as soon as it's celebrated, it leaves your control. It becomes public. In football, this is magnified by the stakes and the media. Whatever we did to win one championship was inevitably going to filter into the plans and strategies of our opponents. (I know this because when other teams would win, we would take *their* best ideas.) But doing the same thing, even if it worked, is going to work less and less in the future, as the pattern of your success—and the jealousy it engenders—spreads out into the wider world.

So what do you do? Throw everything out and start from scratch? We certainly didn't do that. What's the balance between adding too much versus not enough and becoming stagnant?

Finding the balance between knowing what works and trying something new is the secret to handling success. That process begins with *embracing dissatisfaction* (like Pat and Tom) in *pursuit of perfection* (focusing on the errors you made even in the W) and will take you all the way to retirement. Perfection won't be waiting for you there, but more Ws than you ever otherwise would have had will be.

Stay dissatisfied. Stay focused.

In this book I'm telling you about Super Bowl triumphs, signature wins, parades, and other iconic, celebratory moments. The stuff of dreams. So it may come as a surprise that for a chapter on handling success I am going to tell you a story from a significant chunk of my career experience that has rarely been associated with any of that. It will never be captured and sold at memorabilia shows. It's the most boring and insignificant part of the NFL season, often accused of being a money grab by the league, charging premium prices for an inferior product.

It is, of course, preseason football.

But first, some background. In 2001, the Patriots had had numerous outstanding players and rode a late-season wave of tight, low-scoring games to an improbable win in the Super Bowl—a classic fairy-tale season. Some of us, but not many, had won a championship with other teams and we thought we were ready to continue competing. But the following season, 2002, we took a step back and didn't even make the playoffs. (For the record, I never felt that it was because of overconfidence and entitlement. We simply weren't that good. And the competition, especially in our division, had quickly and significantly improved.)

Then, following some good drafts and quality free-agent sign-ings, along with a rock-solid veteran core and a budding star QB now in his third season as the starter, we took a massive jump in 2003. We weren't extraordinary in any one area, but very good in all areas, which meant no real weaknesses—but still, it was the NFL, so we certainly didn't coast in every game. In fact, we were actually in many more close games than you'd expect for an eventual Super Bowl champion with a 17–2 record. We played in ten one-score games and won nine of them (an unheard-of proportion). We had big winning streaks, a shiny record (and a shiny trophy), but that all obscured what really happened on a play-by-play basis that year, because the difference between wins and losses was—and usually is—extremely thin.

A recent comment made by the GOAT of tennis, Roger Federer, sums it up well. Speaking at Dartmouth College's commencement, Federer pointed out a pretty mind-boggling statistic: "In the one thousand five hundred and twenty-six singles matches I played in my career, I won almost eighty percent of those matches. . . . What percentage of points do you think I won in those matches? Only fifty-four percent. In other words, even top-ranked tennis players win barely more than half of the points they play. When you lose every second point on average, you learn not to dwell on every shot."

That margin is everything. It also, mathematically, gets us to the central idea of this chapter. You need to win only 51 percent of a game to come out with 100 percent of a "win." But if you're serious about winning the next one, and the next one after that, you cannot focus on the 51 percent. That's banked. Focus on the 49.

How we think about ourselves in that margin, and what we do there, determines which way things are going to go. That's the way our 2003 Patriots season shook out—very few individual games were lopsided, but the season as a whole was. Team after team played us thinking they had a chance that year, and in a sense, they did. But while Federer's opponents had the edge nearly as often as he did, they stood no chance *when it mattered the most*—and it was the same way for us. We were mentally tougher, made better decisions under pressure, made all the clutch plays. We weren't three, five, or ten games better in terms of talent, but we still walked away with the Ws. They'd shake their heads, lament how close they were, how they should have won, and how they were "right there with the Patriots." But were they?

They weren't and they didn't even know why.

Maybe it was because they didn't handle their relative success very well. Instead of thinking about how close they'd been to a win (even if they were), they should have been focusing on the only thing that could affect their chances moving forward: the 51 percent of the game they'd lost.

Meanwhile, we notched a fifteen-game winning streak. Our last loss had been in September the season before. By the time the next season started, it would have been almost a full calendar year. Now, that's true dominance. *That's* sustained winning.

Fast-forward to the offseason preceding the 2004 season. As a team, we felt there was no reason to be caught off guard about how to approach getting back to the top. (Notice how I put that: getting *back* to the top, and not *staying* on top. We weren't going to stay anywhere. We evaluated what we had, and what we needed, and then we started over.)

The one move that improved us more than any other was adding a new centerpiece to our offense. Corey Dillon was one of the best running backs in the league, but his trade was unexpected, and not entirely well received. In the eyes of many, he was on the downside of his career, and some people had concerns about his character. He was viewed by some as a toxic figure who wouldn't conform to our culture and might even damage it. Those people felt it was an un-Patriots-like move, that acquiring a player with Corey's reputation was what desperate teams did, not champions, and that coaches and general managers did this kind of thing only when they were on the hot seat and willing to sell their standards in exchange for talent (and job security).

I disagreed. Sure, Corey had been frustrated often during his years with the Cincinnati Bengals and made those feelings (potentially overly) clear. But I knew that part of that stemmed from being the best player on a struggling team—and, as a result, a media target. When the Bengals would lose, he'd be the one to have to answer for it the most. I don't know that Corey was necessarily wired for that and at times it showed. But he was a great player, and a very competitive one.

The naysayers didn't understand something essential: we didn't consider ourselves to be "champions" in any meaningful way. We had won the last game. That was done now. Were we "desperate"? No. We were eager to win and committed to adapting our group in the best way possible to do so moving forward. (Emphasis on "moving forward.") Which was what, coincidentally, Corey Dillon did with more ferocity and willfulness than any other running back that season.

When he joined our team, he didn't have to worry about being the face of anything—we already had plenty of those guys. All he had to do was produce. And he did so at a record-setting level. I had a similar experience with Bryan Cox, who was a very good linebacker, tough, and super competitive. He left the Miami Dolphins for Chicago as a free agent and became the best player on a bad defense. His frustration was evident on the field and included some altercations with fans. When he came to the Patriots he could bring his talent and leadership with him but didn't have to stand out and be the face of the franchise. One of my big messages at the start of every training camp, especially when we were expected to be contenders that season, was "We don't have any starters, we don't have any stars." All we had were guys with an opportunity to establish a role or reestablish their level of performance. Was that true? Not entirely. (It would have been hard for me to credibly say Richard Seymour, Ty Law, and a dozen other guys weren't going to be starters. Most of our starting positions were essentially locked up three months before the season began.) But, as the leader of our team, that's not what I talked about. Without misleading anyone, my message was simple: We're all here to compete for a few spots. Yes, some of these guys are really good. So, be better. Everyone is going to be coached.

I can honestly say that our players usually took the message to heart. As they should have. By that point, our track record was clear. Two years earlier, we had traded Drew Bledsoe, the franchise QB with the $100 million contract. One year earlier, we had cut one of the heart and souls of the defense in safety Lawyer Milloy. There was precedent, so how could a player feel completely comfortable that his "starter/star" status was intact? He couldn't. Unless he proved it, again. Just like I had to.

Which brings us back to the excitement of preseason football.

From how I see it, coaches in preseason are always seven months from working their last game. In the offseason, we haven't game planned, we haven't called a play, we haven't made any in-game adjustments. Those are all high-pressure, lightning-speed responsibilities, and you don't just pick up where you left off. You know the feeling of settling back at your desk and opening your email after a long vacation? Multiply that by twenty-five, and replace the emails with linebackers and defensive ends.

Many of you have never watched a complete NFL preseason

game. It takes a special kind of enthusiasm for the league to genuinely enjoy these games, which are really just an opportunity for
players to get back to full physical contact and mentally staying
in a game for sixty minutes, on the field or off, as well as to reestablish fundamentals, timing, and communication. But a successful preseason, arguably, is measured by one factor above all others:
avoiding injury. Nobody plays an entire game; most don't even play
half. In 2023, the average play time for starters was around 10 percent. Several teams didn't play any starters at all during the whole
preseason. So, obviously preseason games aren't anyone's highest
priority, but they can be a key step in a team's progression and I take
them seriously.

Still, I've coached 105 preseason games—the equivalent of six
regular seasons—and 99 percent are forgettable. So that 1 percent
really sticks out.

Patriots at Cincinnati, August 21, 2004, a few months after we
had won our second Super Bowl and established ourselves as a team
to look out for. It was the second preseason game, and the front-line
players were scheduled to play about a quarter—maybe a little into
the second quarter depending on how many possessions there were
to go around. But that's it.

The first quarter consisted of four drives. Two TDs for the Bengals and two three-and-outs for the Patriots. The second quarter
was worse. Those three-and-outs from the first quarter were great
in comparison to the two turnovers in the second quarter. Add another two TDs for the Bengals. Again, this was during the first
half of the game. Our starters were still in. We were getting de-
stroyed, 28–3, and the team on the field consisted of seventeen of
the twenty-two players who led the team onto the field at the Super
Bowl.

I was looking at a team with definite potential for a championship, and equally definite potential to get beaten. Not even *potential* to get beaten, since it was already happening. It was truly embarrassing.

We were a complete no-show. No competitiveness, awareness, communication, execution, or anything else you need to win *any* game, much less follow up on our Super Bowl win with continuing success. We were playing inadequate, noncompetitive football. It wasn't just on the players. We were obviously poorly coached that night—we weren't prepared and couldn't do anything right. It's long been said that it's easier to get to the top than it is to stay there. That night in Cincinnati, I was certain that staying there wouldn't just be hard. It might be impossible.

I had a choice to make. I could continue pleading with the guys to put last year behind them and find a way to get hungry for the next one. Or I could do something about it. Since they had clearly already ignored my warnings, I decided against more talk. Instead, I kept playing 'em. I was most upset by the attitude of the team. The majority of the starting players didn't want to play and didn't care that we were noncompetitive. I thought that risked becoming a bad habit (and bad habits are hard to break), so I told the players that they were going to play until they started competing.

They played past halftime, and they played through the third quarter. Starters from a Super Bowl–winning team, playing deep into a preseason game . . . it was unthinkable. It was probably longer than many of them had played in a preseason game since their rookie years. Dillon carried the football. Willie McGinest, Richard Seymour, and Ty Law all kept going, shocked, making tackles, making plays. And, believe me, they were not happy about playing three quarters of the second preseason game.

Was I concerned about one of them being injured? Yes and no. Yes, because I never want to see anyone hurt. No, because as much of a detriment as it might be for our team to lose any one of those guys, their complacency would hurt our team more. So I willingly risked these guys in the second half of a preseason game. This team was loaded with Pro Bowlers, All-Pros, eventual Patriots Hall of Famers and Pro Football Hall of Famers. And as experienced, mature, and celebrated as they were, they just didn't get it. You can have all the healthy and talented players you want, but if they aren't doing anything the way they're supposed to, it means nothing. No matter what you do, no matter what you've accomplished, none of us is far away from coasting. Give me hungry rookies instead.

What would have happened if any of those starters had been seriously injured because I left them in a "meaningless" game? I'd have been crushed by media and fans. But games are only meaningless to people who aren't in them. That night wasn't just a preseason game, and I made sure the team eventually understood that.

I'd be stretching it to say that that decision was the reason we started the season 6–0, set an NFL record with twenty-one straight wins, finished the season 14–2, and won another Super Bowl.

But it is the reason we were prepared to do so. We handled our success by staying in the present moment, which, in Cincinnati, was bad. We didn't look backward at our accomplishments, or talk about being in the Super Bowl, which was months away. In order to get to a championship game, the team had to navigate over a hundred days of practice and preparation and *earn* the right to play in important games.

I've had a couple models for how to handle success in my own career. The first one is obvious, but the story is worth telling again. When I first met Tom Brady, he was just out of college and looked the part. (You've probably seen the picture of Tom at the combine—yup, that one, where he looks about as athletic as a junior high equipment manager.) As for me, I had darker hair, and more of it, and a few less wrinkles. A middle-aged guy with young kids. Both of us had some experience winning, but not in a fully formed way. He was a sophomore on the bench during the 1997 Michigan championship season, while I coordinated the defense for the Giants during two Super Bowl wins, in 1987 and 1991. In the grand scheme of things, both of us could hold our heads high: we had played roles on winning teams. We both could have retired and cut some commercials for car dealerships and local chambers of commerce. Tom would probably have become the athletic director at Michigan, or a senator, and I'd have had a biweekly segment on WFAN to complain about the Knicks.

But obviously that wasn't going to be enough. For either of us.

There were any number of times during the Patriots years when it would have made some kind of sense for us to take our feet off the accelerator. I'm sure plenty of NFL fans (and NFL teams) would have supported us in doing that. After that first Super Bowl in 2002, we were "made men" in many respects—that year, U2, at the peak of their fame, had been picked to play the halftime show, and when we ran into them during media appearances, Bono and the Edge were asking *us* about our personnel decisions. The 9/11 attacks had occurred only months before, and the Patriots' story and spirit of resilience became a rallying call for people all over the world who were determined to stand tall in the face of violence and terrorism. We were world-famous, and that was *before* we stepped onto the field and won that game literally against all odds.

We easily could have walked into the sunset. Or more realistically, if we had never won another Super Bowl together, I feel confident that that one in New Orleans would have been remembered forever and cemented our place in NFL history. People love underdogs, and that's what we were, once upon a time. But an obsession with winning kept us going, and it never crossed our minds to stop.

It's a lesson I learned from my father, Steve, my other model for how to handle success. He was already a winning football man when he joined the staff at the Naval Academy in 1956, but success in those days didn't necessarily come with the big bucks that coaches earn today. He got a nice raise to $5,600 a year when he moved from the University of North Carolina at Chapel Hill up to Annapolis, but an aversion to credit of any kind kept a lid on our standard of living. He was like a lot of men and women who grew up poor and lived through the Depression—every cent got counted, and the things that mattered most were real and tangible. He saved money more than he spent, even as he accrued greater success, and greater influence, in his career, driving himself around during his scouting trips and keeping the receipts. He made sure he was treated fairly. As a young boy, I was occasionally envious of the families who were a bit more liberal in their spending habits, but I mostly took it as a natural fact of life that we conserved, we saved, and we maintained. (When I say we "maintained" I mean that in the literal sense of the word: we cared for and fixed things around the house, like our clothes and appliances.) And that maintenance, though I didn't realize it at the time, ensured that we rose in the world. A commitment to saving was a commitment to building a future for his children, and his children's children.

He was not unique, and I am not claiming otherwise. Many people in his generation (my parents belonged to Tom Brokaw's "Greatest Generation") and many more today, especially in some immigrant communities, prioritized saving money and preparing for the future, whatever it might hold (perhaps it's no coincidence that I ended up in New England, the ancestral home of "waste not, want not" and what used to be called Yankee thrift). While my father grew as a man and as a football scout and coach, he never grew out of this mindset. If I ever chafed under this as a child, I now deeply admire it. He was not changed by his success because he was *ready* for his success. And when it came, he did not assume that it would be fleeting, nor did he think of himself as lucky to achieve it.

Winning does not mean spending or cashing out what you earn. When your first win comes, celebrate it, but take some time to practice some restraint.

And remember: that Bentley looks good on the lot, but the average NFL career lasts less than four years, and that rookie signing bonus isn't nearly as big after taxes, especially in Massachusetts.

ONE GOOD OUTCOME DOESN'T MEAN ANYTHING. THE ONLY SUCCESS THAT

MATTERS IS SUSTAINED SUCCESS. EMBRACE DISSATISFACTION.

FIVE

ROSTER CONSTRUCTION

O f everything involved with building your team, two priorities are at the very top. First: knowing what you want. Second: superbly evaluating what you already have.

Good roster construction is a tricky balance between the overall team vision and the people who must carry out that vision. One cannot work without the other. If you are a leader, you manage that balance by scouting and developing talent that matches the vision. If you are a member of the team, you must understand how you fit in, be honest about what your own strengths are, and find ways to make yourself invaluable to the overall vision.

Roster construction involves managing the push and pull of how individuals fit into groups, how groups can serve individuals, and how everyone can serve a common goal. For me, roster construction can be summed up best by something researcher and consultant Jim Collins said in his book *Good to Great*: "Get the right people on the bus." I have never told a personnel manager that I didn't want a good player because he didn't fit our system. If the personnel department got me a good player, it was my responsibility to have a broad-enough system in order to use him well.

The first day I walked into the Browns' offices in Berea, Ohio, in 1991, I told pro personnel director Michael Lombardi about my vision for a football team. "We are building a big, physical football team from the inside out. We will be strong down the middle and be able to play in any weather conditions. We want players who are tough, smart, and dependable." Michael started his search for players who met this criteria. We made some refinements along the way, but the point was to start with a plan, take action to execute the plan, and not get distracted from the plan. As a leader, a big part of my responsibility has always been to communicate my vision to other people, so that they in turn can help make that vision real.

Talent is necessary but not sufficient for the purpose of putting together a great team. I've seen teams with lots of talent fail to come together or achieve anything because they stayed siloed like a fantasy football roster. Just like a new apartment complex will have both an architect and a management company, an organization built to prosper will be attentive to its raw materials and output *as well as* its coherence and attractiveness as a unit. Collecting talent is different from building a team. The goal is to build a team, but collecting the *right* talent comes first.

That begins with an informed, specific goal. Don't assume that the team will join together under a vision once they're all in the mix—make them part of it from the start. The more vivid the vision, the more vivid the path will appear. That path will help you build. And win. It needs to be rendered as precisely as possible, and consider *your* objectives, not the needs or demands of others outside the organization.

You have to know your team's identity and therefore what—and who—will mesh with that identity, extend it, enhance it, even challenge it in constructive ways. At our best, the Patriots identity was all about *details*.

Before Tom Brady was clearly the greatest QB of all time, he was still seen (with some justification) as having gaps in his game. He didn't put up numbers like Dan Marino or Brett Favre or Randall Cunningham; he didn't have the pedigree. So what explained his ability—and then, as a result, our team's ability—to win? A resolute focus on the details of the game.*

It wasn't an accident that Brady ended up on our team. From our earliest era of success, our team vision was to find players who knew how to execute the in-between game. We wanted players who embraced performing in ways that wouldn't necessarily be accounted for in any stat, but would certainly be noticed by the coaches—getting out-of-bounds to stop the clock instead of picking up a couple more yards, or spreading the ball around as a QB to keep as many people engaged as possible, or finding a way as a linebacker of muddying up receiver routes. These actions are things you might not get immediately paid for, but they contribute to the win. I call it "playing smart football." How do you identify prospects who will do the inglorious things?

If there is one word to describe this general topic, it's "maturity." A mature person will be able to handle whatever gets thrown at them, good or bad. Every player will find failure (and usually at

---

* The truth was we had a lot of players like that, except most of them were veterans like McGinest and Vrabel and Bruschi—guys who were certainly very good but didn't rank as "great" to many analysts of the game. This kind of distinction, though, is, frankly, lost on me. Good players become great players when they match with a system that enhances their ability to be productive. I like to think about what a player *can* do, not what he *cannot* do. We, as coaches, should try to keep a player out of compromising situations.

THE ART OF WINNING

least a degree of success) in his field. His maturity is a good indicator of how he will take that success in stride and how he will navigate adversity and remain competitive. Most players deal with common setbacks involving injuries, playing time, coaching criticism, and negative fan reaction, as well as (sometimes unrealistically) high expectations. How will he handle them?

We find the right players by looking for people who have good overall abilities, who have a *range* of abilities, and who are confident enough to perform a task that isn't exactly matched up with their strength. When I say that I look for football intelligence (FBI), or just intelligent players, period, I'm not talking about IQ tests and degrees. It's what shows up in a player's capacity to do many things well enough. In casual speech, that sometimes gets boiled down to "having humility" or even more simply "being a team player." That's probably effective as a rule of thumb. But just remember: When you're trying to find these kinds of people, it's not about their eagerness to be sociable and have fun. That comes after winning. The best players for our system will always be most mindful of winning, and let that lead them wherever it goes. For someone like Troy Brown, that meant becoming an all-around player, catching passes, returning punts, and playing cornerback when necessary. The ultimate importance of Troy wasn't that he added this or that much expected value in those different roles; it was more fundamental than that.

I don't need to overexplain why it's good when players can do these in-between things, but I do need to make clear the benefit: when players see other players doing these "small" things, it generates trust. Troy put winning first. His teammates could tell. And that made them want to put winning first too.

That's not to say I am suggesting you select potential above all else—in fact, it's critically important that new teammates are clearly excellent in some way. But that excellence doesn't necessarily need to be conspicuous. Look for excellence on the margins. Look where other people aren't looking. Great teammates embrace competition internally and externally. We prepared to face elite opponents by competing against each other to improve our performance and sharpen our skills. Brady, Julian Edelman, Harrison, Vrabel, Bruschi, Slater, Keenan McCardell, and Anthony Pleasant were all great practice players who did not start their career as stars. They outworked their teammates and opponents on and off the field to achieve success. After establishing themselves as great players, they embraced the competition from teammates who would push them to higher performance levels.

Yes, we all want a team full of elite prospects. We want the smartest, fastest, strongest, and most reliable options out there. But those are just paper stats, and they can never be the basis for selecting your guys. Your competitors have the same info. They see the same test scores, the same résumés, the same names. No great team was ever assembled like a Pro Bowl. That's why we don't just ask, "Who's the best?" We ask: "Who's the best for *us*?"

To find out, we teach our coaches how to be scouts. But before they ever set foot on a field, we need to make sure everyone is on the same page. Part of this is learning how to write reports and how to follow a unified approach to evaluations. We all have to know the vision and where we need help to fulfill it. We must all use the same language and terminology so that even if we have different opinions on a player, we know what we are disagreeing about. The key to good evaluations is to establish the criteria we are looking for and have the evaluators be consistent in their grades. As Michael Lombardi would always tell me, it's critically important to "evaluate the evaluators." If the evaluator is inaccurate or sloppy (for whatever reason), the evaluation is borderline useless.

Every evaluation consists of major factors like size, speed, explosion, instincts, and position specifics. For a receiver, specifics apply to the skills we look for at his position, such as the ability to separate, blocking, hands, football intelligence, etc. The scout includes the player's strong points, weak points, and a summary. Finally, the evaluator puts a grade and his opinion on the prospect: What will he be for our team?

That is the line that really matters. Is he a starter, backup, rotational player? Will he bring leadership, toughness, and football intelligence to the team? Will he be a good teammate? The final opinion is what the player *will be*, not what he was somewhere else. This is the hardest but most important part to get right. Lots of evaluators can point out what someone has already accomplished. The hard part is to project what he will do in the future.

In the end the answer is one of these three: *Yes*, this player will help us win championships. *No*, we don't want the player for any combination of reasons. Or *maybe*, meaning that we want to work with this player because of his potential and upside, but cannot say at this time that he belongs in the top category. If we identify a player as one who we want on our team, the next step is to determine how good he is and what his draft value or free-agency price might be. Ultimately, we want to draft or sign as many "yes" players as possible, players who will help us win, and then as many "maybe" players as possible, players who *might* help us if they pan out or develop to their full potential. Ultimately, to have a complete roster, the bottom of the roster may have some "no" players, players who we don't expect to make the team but are low-maintenance and will compete.

Don't overlook those "maybe" and "no" players. They might just be in between the roles in which they can thrive. For many players, the in-between stop in their career is the practice squad, where a team can evaluate him and move him onto the roster when he is ready to help the team. For a staff member, the in-between stop could be an intern type of position so that you can evaluate the employee.

Still, rather than hiring a "maybe" to a full-time position, potentially creating a situation where he will later have to be released, I liked to soften the commitment and essentially say to the player: "Prove it." If the new hire works out, he can be elevated to a full-time position. If the new hire falls short of expectations, I would replace him with another intern and hope for better results.

When you bring someone into the organization, you're getting their total package. You can't ignore something just because you don't like it or think it will be washed away by the good things. Someone could easily have great potential on the field but fail to match what we're trying to build. Conversely, he could be an incredible human being: intelligent, unselfish, hardworking. But does he truly love the work? Is it evident in his preparation level? Is this someone I want in my foxhole? When we lose a couple of games, how will he handle it? How does he interact with support people? Don't only tell me what he is today—he may be decent or even good right now. But what's he going to be next year? How about in three to five years? What's the growth trajectory projection? (And this is no one-shot deal. Our standards adjust from year to year according to the current landscape. Ten or twenty years ago, we had projected which players would be good fullbacks in our system. Now the fullback position barely exists. Are you ahead or on schedule with your industry's trends? Are you playing catch-up?) This is massively important. We were fortunate in New England. Some of our rosters were among the oldest in the league. That's fine if you're winning championships, but you better be building up your young core as you go. Do not be too quick to dismiss a player's value or too focused on what he cannot do. What *can* he do that may have value to the team?

Books have been written about Tom Brady's many strengths (and I think more should be written), but one that I wish would get more attention is his ability to make decisions. To me, that was the greatest of all his great strengths. To process the movements of twenty-one bodies moving at peak speed, to gather information from them, and to make a judgment based on that information—while massive, ferocious men are in hot pursuit—is truly demanding work. An example of elite football intelligence.

But there's another player who contributed enormously to our team and who may not have been the most obvious choice for it. In 2017, a couple days before he made one of the most spectacular catches in Super Bowl history and helped his team come back and win from being down, 28–3, Julian Edelman was in an alley outside our hotel in Houston. It was 6 a.m. He was doing a tennis ball drill, along with an unlucky assistant equipment manager he'd dragged out of bed.

The drill is simple enough in theory, but incredibly challenging in practice: the assistant stands a few feet away from Julian and tosses balls at him from various release points. It keeps his reach time and hand-eye coordination at peak levels. For years, he did it every day for thirty minutes.

By 2017, Julian was an established veteran, a terrific receiver, and a proven winner. He didn't have to be down in that alley. No one told him to go down there. But Julian understood the principle of No Days Off, because Julian had not always been a terrific receiver—before we had scouted and drafted him, as a matter of fact, he hadn't been a receiver, period. He was a quarterback out of a small school, and a seventh-round draft pick. Julian was a total projection. He played QB at Kent State, but in the NFL, he was a receiver and punt returner. Edelman's two primary positions were totally new to him. Later in his career, he added a third position: slot cornerback. Talk about embracing change and being comfortable being uncomfortable, Julian was Exhibit A.

If we had gone strictly by the stats and paperwork, he might never have been a Patriot. But our evaluation process revealed a determination to learn, a commitment to personal self-betterment, an intense competitiveness (often against himself), a toughness to persevere through countless injuries and setbacks, and, obviously, an exemplary athletic ability. Those things brought Julian to our team, and down into that alley. And soon after, they were on full display as he held on to a tipped ball for a first down, surrounded by three Atlanta defenders furiously trying to rip it away from him.

That's the kind of player we were looking for, and that's the kind of player we saw. When you evaluate and select according to your standard, your standard will only get better and better.

We developed six categories that we applied to every player we considered pursuing for the Patriots. I am sharing them here because every job requires specific and sometimes unique skills. I strongly believe that these categories can be applied in almost any domain with some reasonable modifications. Some of the philosophies or approaches might surprise you, but they've worked beautifully for us.

BEHAVIORAL CHARACTER

The question that I want answered about any prospective player or employee is simply: How important is football to the individual?

Do they love football? I know that I'm going to have to deal with some maintenance from time to time—if you're looking for fifty-three model citizens or fifty-three model *anythings*, who also perform at an elite level, you'll be looking forever.

One of the first things we need to understand about a guy is what's under the helmet. We need to find out who this person really is and what drives him. What kind of teammate will he be? Just like a vision needs detail, so does a behavioral profile. I tell my scouts, "Don't describe a player with a generic 'clean' or 'not a good program fit' and leave it at that." Tell me why. Our scouts need to be detectives and find out more about the prospective player *before* he comes into our organization. If the player is a good teammate and respected by his coaches, that will carry more weight than any disciplinary report. I really want to know if he is a good *teammate* and his team accepts him, more than I want to know if he ever got into trouble somewhere else. That said, we do not want players who have issues with authority. Do not try to overanalyze this, because every case is different. Our job openings aren't normal and they aren't for normal people—sometimes we have to bend a little, consciously, for exceptional performers.

ATHLETIC ABILITY

I know everything a football player needs to know and I work hard, but nobody wants to see *me* running around out there. Certain baseline athletic standards must be met. At the same time, we need *football players*, not just strong, fast guys. Troy Brown is one of the best receivers to ever play for the Patriots, but not because of his timed speed. His combination of quickness, balance, body control, change of direction, and sense of timing and spatial relationships made him special. Talent is good, but functional talent is great. In the end, I have to feel good that the player can compete with the other players at his position. When I looked at a linebacker who had a thousand tackles in college, I still had to picture that player next to our players such as Dont'a Hightower, Jamie Collins, Rob Ninkovich, Kyle Van Noy, and Elandon Roberts. If I couldn't realistically envision the player I was evaluating as having any chance to compete with our players, I probably wouldn't take him.

STRENGTH AND EXPLOSION

Do not confuse weight room numbers with play strength and power. We aren't just looking for people who can lift hundreds of pounds; we're looking for people who know how to really *use* their strength. I've seen players set strength-training records, but when placed on a football field with twenty-one other players, they get tossed around the field by guys who can't move nearly as much weight on a bar. The sooner we know that, the less likely we are to find ourselves depending on that weight room warrior. We need to know how well a person's pure strength correlates to what we need him to accomplish. One of the most important fundamentals in football is a player's ability to deliver a blow on the move and to be able to defend himself *against* a blow on the move, and no squat or bench number can help us evaluate whether he can or can't. The ability to deal with contact on the move can be recognized in his balance, explosion, and leverage—more than in the weight he can lift in a stationary position.

COMPETITIVENESS

Success in anything requires competitiveness, and we see that trait most clearly in how we prepare and perform. Intensity, work ethic, focus are all part of our competitive nature. Do you play up to your competition? Do you play down to it? Do you just get through practice and mundane aspects of your job and think you can show up on game day ready to surpass high-level competition? Or do you approach every meeting, practice, and game as opportunities to improve? We want guys who have a true, natural desire to win. Otherwise, what are we all doing here? When players have a similar level of ability, I would always take the more competitive person.

TOUGHNESS

Physical toughness may not be as critical in most lines of work, but I can't imagine one not needing mental toughness. You better know how to assess it too. Has he or she ever quit anything? How has he dealt with adversity? Is she self-motivated? Will he push himself or does he need a daily pep talk? How disciplined is he in every aspect of his preparation? Does he put on a good show when the boss is watching or is he just as good when nobody is watching? What is his capacity for pushing through tough times or when he feels like giving up? To get where we want, there's going to be pressure. Around sixty-five thousand people will be watching in person and another fifteen million watching on TV. He will get knocked down, one way or the other. How will he get back up?

Mental toughness is doing the right things for the team when everything isn't perfect for you.

LEARNING

Intelligence takes many forms. I have coached players with a first-grade reading level who could come off a football field and rattle off a dozen things that just took place with mind-blowing insights. And I have coached highly intelligent college graduates who couldn't tell you what the guy lined up five feet across from him just did, in football terms. Do not assume your smartest prospect will be your top producer. He may be your most frustrating. Players with below-average FBI will not be successful in our program because (1) our system requires the ability to process information and communicate and (2) they will eventually make dumb mistakes. We assess this based on the types of questions he asks and whether he is an error repeater. How well does he communicate with teammates, in meetings, and on the field? Is he a student of the game? And does he even want to be?

Unfortunately, roster construction doesn't just involve addition.

Be ready to replace the key people in your organization. You can anticipate employees leaving your organization when you are successful. Josh McDaniels was ready to take over as offensive coordinator when Charlie Weis left for Notre Dame after the 2005 season. Bill O'Brien was prepared to take over for Josh when McDaniels became the head coach of the Denver Broncos after the 2009 season. Joe Judge was set to take over as special teams coordinator when Scott O'Brien retired. Readiness can be just as effective as continuity, if you have the right people in the building and a clear vision for who might join them. I felt that if a promising young player's progress was being blocked, I had to clear the way for the young player to emerge. My choice was to either trade or release the player who was (probably unintentionally) in the path of the promising young player.

Moving on from good, productive, and loyal players was, by far, the hardest part of my job. I had to balance loyalty to the player with the future of the team. What was the value of a player compared to the value we could get without that player? Before releasing any player, you must know what value he brings to the team. During my time as a coach, I had an abundance of players who I really wanted on the team but financially could not keep: Lawyer Milloy, Tom Brady, Adam Vinatieri, Willie McGinest, Vince Wilfork, Mike Vrabel, Joe Thuney, Deion Branch, Logan Mankins, Darrelle Revis, Aqib Talib, Ty Law, and Nate Solder to name a few. I wanted those players and many others who ultimately were not affordable under the Patriots' salary cap. Another consideration is that some good players are better fits in different schemes or situations—these are trade opportunities that potentially help both teams. It was along those lines that I acquired a number of players through the years who became major contributors for the Patriots: players like Dillon, Randy Moss, Van Noy, Ted Washington, and Wes Welker. And I traded some players who fit better in other schemes, like Eric Metcalf and Drew Bledsoe. Unfortunately, I allowed a couple of young, affordable players to get away, such as placekicker Robbie Gould. If after a full season of working with your team on a daily basis, you make a mistake on what you have, or don't have, you have hurt the team. I never wanted to do that. Ultimately, these hard and crucial decisions have to be made, but they can be gut-wrenching.

Roster change is not always a bad thing—just have a plan. If you hire someone from outside your organization for a high-level position, expect to make modifications in policy and other personnel in that department when the new boss implements some changes. If you don't like the idea of an outsider leading, then make sure you have a replacement well trained to take over.

As an employee, you should observe and learn from your boss. How can I do my job better for him? What is he doing well and not so well as my superior? When you get an opportunity to move up, be prepared. That is your job: be ready to take advantage of an opportunity in your career path. Don't expect anyone else to do that for you. If you have a mentor, that's great. I wouldn't count on it. People above you have full-time jobs, and may not have time to train you. If you want to advance, start training yourself!

In my first five years as an NFL coach, I had the good fortune to be around many great teachers and coaches with an outstanding work ethic. I also was around some coaches who were not consistently prepared and cut corners that decreased their production. In fact, they were letting their team down and I didn't respect them, even though I worked for them. I never wanted anyone to think of me as someone who let the team down.

STEVE BELICHICK

If my father, Steve Belichick, were alive today, he would be 106 years old. Page 106 seems like the right spot to pay tribute to him.

My dad was raised during hard times in this country. To have a chance at success, he had to do a lot of things properly, and he did. One thing he did right was to marry my mom, Jeannette. Steve's life revolved around football. Football gave him the opportunity to go to college, to be a naval officer, and to coach. He genuinely loved his players—sometimes it was a tough love—and they loved him. He was a teacher, but he also learned from his players.

In 1966, my dad started the Chesapeake Football Camp with Jack Cloud, another assistant coach at Navy. The camp was all football—and it was tough. The staff trained the kids twice a day. The campers paid $400 for a week of sprints, monkey rolls in the mud, and the very best football fundamentals and techniques.

When he retired, he became a painter—my mom gave him the perfect Christmas present in 1985. She gave him a paint set, an easel, and a blank canvas. She had seen some of his drawings from high school and thought that he would enjoy painting—she was so right! Twenty years later, he finished dozens of paintings, and gave most of them away to his friends.

Dad, thank you for taking care of me and sharing your passion for football. We have shared your wisdom through a couple of generations to thousands of players and coaches, and a growing family.

You are the trunk of the tree and we are the branches. Thank you for inspiring us, and for making our lives richer. I think about you every day.

YOUR VISION MUST PRECEDE YOUR ROSTER. IDENTIFY WHAT TRAITS YOU ARE LOOKING FOR BEFORE YOU BEGIN LOOKING. AS AN EMPLOYEE, MAKE YOURSELF A BETTER FIT BY OBSERVING WHAT LEADERS IN YOUR ORGANIZATION ARE SEEKING. BUY INTO THE CORE VALUES OF THE PROGRAM.

SIX

STAR PLAYERS

This chapter is about the elite performers and how to handle them. To be clear, the challenges that sometimes come along with stars are good challenges to have. A singular talent can be the final piece of a championship team. Elite results come from elite performers, and elite performers must have elite talent.

Unfortunately, talent isn't distributed how we might like it to be. Some people have a lot of it, but they never get a chance to know it or exercise it because no one ever gives them a shot. Maybe they look the wrong way or were born in the wrong place. Maybe they weren't raised right. For some, it's situational. Some people, however, have a lot of talent but no discipline to speak of.

Discipline alone can't win championships, but it *can* turn elite talent into elite performance. It *can* be the difference between being in the starting lineup and sitting on the bench. Discipline shows up. Discipline is ready to go. Disciplined players don't pull their hamstrings because they are dehydrated from drinking at the bar or club. Disciplined workers don't fall asleep in meetings because they stayed up all night playing *Capture the Flag* on their Sony War Hero in their hotel room. Discipline comes in numerous forms. Great players will check every box: discipline to train, to practice, to study, and to prepare. Discipline is doing the right thing every time, and not just when someone is looking. Do you put the shopping cart back in the stall? Do you do it even if you're the last one in the parking lot?

Case in point: Rodney Harrison. Rodney was entering his tenth season when we signed him. He was one of the best safeties in the NFL, a feared hitter the likes of which the league hadn't seen in a long time. Rodney was an All-Pro and a Pro Bowler as a San Diego Charger—an elite player by any definition. But when you're among the most physical players out there, your body has absorbed as much impact as you've dished out. He was coming off a significant groin injury and was on the wrong side of thirty; most people seemed to think he had lost a step. But that criticism was disingenuous. His game had never just been based on having blazing speed. He was elite because he was so much more.

When I think about Rodney, I think about intensity, intimidation, communication, flexibility. But, more than anything, two words come to mind: scout team.

In the NFL, the scout team is a group of eleven players who, essentially, play the role of our opponents in a practice. They simulate the plays and approaches teams might take against us so that we're prepared for any situation. The idea dates back to Cleveland's legendary coach Paul Brown, who had some developmental players who weren't good enough to make the team but who he knew would be beneficial to keep around—the team would have more bodies to run plays, and if the player took the training and eventually earned himself a roster spot, they retained that talent. The only problem was that the league had a roster limit rule. Only so many names could be active.

As a creative workaround, Coach Brown asked the Browns' owner, Arthur McBride, to hire the developmental guys as employees at the taxicab company he owned so they wouldn't be in violation of any roster requirements. (Hence the original name for the group—"the taxi squad.") McBride agreed. Those "cabdrivers" became the foundation of the practice squad strategy. To this day, we still seek out exactly those kinds of guys. It's a win-win situation: they help us practice, and they get to be seen every day by pro scouts and coaches. It's not a star-studded group, but that's the point. Most of our rostered players wouldn't think about ever joining a scout team to give us some useful competition. And I wouldn't begrudge them that.

But that was the thing about Rodney: he demanded to play on the scout team. Even I was a little surprised. Here's this all-time talent at safety, a man who has probably hit more guys (and hit them harder) than almost anyone else, and he's signing up for the most thankless job in practice.

There's a term in baseball—"eyewash"—for when guys try to look like they're working extra hard or giving more to the team than they actually are. It happens in football too. Fake hustle. Rodney volunteering to run down on kickoff coverage on the scout team just to give our starters an actual challenge in practice, so that they could raise their games . . . is the opposite of eyewash. He made the starters better, he made the other guys on the scout team better, and he made the coaches better. Not only that, but his scout team play also kept him in peak condition during the season.

Some people elevate their peers simply by their daily example. Or their reputation. With Rodney, everything he did was elevating.

Elite players do more than what they are merely required to do, and that kind of behavior isn't just nice to see from time to time, or good for show. It uplifts everyone else's game. I would be willing to bet that your best performers aren't just doing what's marked as "mandatory" in the employee handbook. Elite players want to win. Elite talent wants success, and so they will do whatever needs to be done to create and exist in an environment where it's possible.

In a paper published by the National Bureau of Economic Research in 2014, the economists Casey Ichniowski and Anne Preston studied the effect of "star performers" on their teammates, specifically when it came to top-level European soccer clubs. One of the key takeaways?

> The empirical results consistently show that performance improves more after an individual has been a member of an elite team than when he has been a member of lower level teams.

That's right. The authors found that in situation after situation players raised their games, permanently, when they saw elite performances from elite peers. Ichniowski, who was himself an award-winning youth soccer coach, also included some excerpts from interviews with the players:

> You also see that it's how you live and your attitude toward how you spend your time away from the training so you're ready to train. . . . Right next to me, I had [list of four internationally acclaimed internationals from other countries]. I saw right in front of me how it was done. They were mentors right in front of you to watch.

Not tape or coaching or raw talent. Those players knew they'd become better—that they'd become winners—because the people around them set a bar and they had no choice but to reach it. Elite players like Rodney Harrison make other players better. They know it. They bring models, mentorship, and motivation. If you manage them correctly—and if you lead them—they will in turn lead the rank and file. Without elite performers, the teams I've coached never would have won anything.

As important as elite players are, if they can't be managed well, they'll just bring headaches. In 2019 we signed the unbelievably talented wide receiver Antonio Brown the day before our final preseason game. He would last thirteen days as a Patriot.

The reaction to our signing Antonio was . . . mixed. In some circles, there was an excitement I hadn't seen since we had signed another star receiver and erstwhile Oakland Raider, Randy Moss, in 2007 (Moss had elite talent and eventually transformed our offense). Others, though, had serious objections to working with someone with baggage—especially when that baggage included publicly feuding with team brass. Once he came on board, every one of those thirteen days was full of debate and noise about Antonio and his fitness as a Patriot, and both sides were equally loud. Of all the players I have ever coached, not one has inspired the same spectrum of reaction over such a short time.

Of course, one person I could rely on to keep an even keel was Tom Brady. The ultimate leader, he knew right away that if anyone could settle Antonio down and integrate him and his talent into our team concept, it would be a quarterback with six Super Bowl rings. There was something else that connected the two players: both had been sixth-round draft picks who had become superstars. It also helped that apart from all his theatrics, Antonio was a very smart player and picked up on our offense right away. He was driven and worked hard, which Tom respected. The two of them established a close relationship very quickly, sharing a similarly intense commitment to training, and bonding over idiosyncrasies. (And oh, were there idiosyncrasies.)

Something I think it's important to say up front: every player has his quirks. We're dealing with individuals, after all, and though someone can be singularly focused on winning, there are sometimes different paths to how they get there or how they channel their emotions and actions.

I remember one time in particular, when Antonio decided to give Tom a gift. This by itself wasn't uncommon; players often give each other gifts like jewelry, electronics, clothing, or even vacations. But not Antonio.

Instead of any of those things, he gave Tom milk and bison. Perhaps Antonio had perceived in Tom a kindred spirit on the subject of nutrition. By then Tom's fixation on diet was widely known. He had actually just gifted his new teammate some of his TB12-branded water. Hence the milk and meat.

But not the kind you and I might drink. Not from a grocery store. No, this was special milk. Very special. Flown in from the Midwest. It had nutritional superpowers, and it certainly should have because it apparently cost over $500 a bottle. Antonio had several bottles of this magic milk shipped to Foxborough on the Friday before our first road game in Miami. The only problem was that due to a mix-up on when and where the presentation would be coordinated, the delivery arrived at Tom's locker late in the afternoon and there was no marking on the box to indicate the contents were perishable. Even Antonio's magic milk couldn't survive spending a night next to Tom's locker at room temperature. It was spoiled, and right before we were about to hit the road.

Antonio was hurt and frustrated that his special gift had been ruined, and Tom felt bad because his friend felt bad, and our staff was walking on eggshells. On top of that, somehow the chain of custody for this magic milk had ended with the Patriots staff, so we were responsible for the whole mess. It was the eve of a game that we had been working toward for weeks, and now our emotions and equilibrium had been thrown out of whack. The gift had been a genuine attempt at some team bonding on Antonio's part, but now we were all crying over spoiled milk. Unfortunately, it fell to me to arrange with an understandably skeptical business office at the Patriots the need for reimbursement, and quickly. (Imagine having to be the person saying this on a professional phone call: "So, look, I'll preface this with . . . yes, I know this is hard to believe, but it's Tom, it's AB, they've got a kind of football bromance thing going on right now. . . . If it were anyone else, I'd for sure tell them to get lost, but we should do this. Yes, I know it's thirty-five hundred dollars for groceries.")

It was the last thing I wanted to deal with, but leaders don't necessarily get to pick and choose what they get called in for. Our staff had their hands full dealing with our trip to Miami, so I had to do what I needed to do to get us back on track. Think about it this way: Would you spend $3,500 dollars to ensure the best person on your team gave their best performance when it mattered most? Would you pay twice that to immediately relieve your star employee of a depressive episode, no matter how head-shaking? Absolutely, and you know it. Your job is not to psychoanalyze. Your job is to put people in a position to win.

We made it to the game, and 2019 was the last time the Patriots won in Miami, thanks in part to Antonio's touchdown.

Ultimately, the milk and meat turned out to be the least of Antonio's problems, and his Miami debut was also his finale as a Patriot. We released him a few days later. Signing him definitely was not worth the millions we owed him in signing bonus payments, but I don't regret buying that milk. And it all seemed to work out. A couple of years later, Antonio and Tom rekindled their football marriage in Tampa Bay and won a Super Bowl. Antonio had five receptions and a touchdown. Maybe the milk works.

The lesson here is that elite players, star performers, and top talent are a critical part of a winning team, but critical doesn't mean simple. The best of the best can either multiply their talents and make everyone else better or they can drag everyone else down. The biggest mistake you can make (besides never finding any elite talent in the first place) is thinking you must dominate them and force them to fit into a mold you've already established. Elite talent should inspire new visions and possibilities and make you reconsider what your game plan might look like.

People are different. People have different opinions, different tastes, different politics, and different levels of tolerance for pain and discomfort. Those are all factors you must manage and lead. You must decide what is nonnegotiable. The nonnegotiable stuff was encoded in our basic principles: Do Your Job, No Days Off, and others. If you've set up your organization in the right way, your employees should thrive, and that thriving should all add up to big team wins. Your job isn't to make everyone who works for you conform to some code of life. Leave that to their families and faiths. Every football team I've ever been a part of has been composed of a group of men who would only ever find themselves in the same place at the same time for two reasons: football, and the desire to win. That's more than enough glue to hold everything together.

Once more, because it's a truth worth underscoring: a championship team needs to have some elite talent. In order for the team to sustain a high level of performance, that talent has to be an amplifier and not a detractor. That means you have to look deeper than the résumé and the reputation. If you ever have the opportunity to hire an elite performer who has supposedly "lost a step," look past the numbers and see what kind of teammate he'll be. His impact on instilling a winning atmosphere might more than make up for whatever decline you can measure on paper.

And finally, remember to mark perishable packages.

In approximately five billion years, we are all cooked. That is when scientists predict the sun will run out of hydrogen and start to collapse in on itself at its core, even as the outermost surface will be pushed outward and engulf several planets in our solar system, including the one that you and I currently occupy. At that point, any remaining trace of human life will be washed away in some kind of cosmic tidal wave. No more quarterly earnings, no more P&L statements, no more Thursday-night games on short rest, no more combine scouting reports. Perhaps by then we'll have fired off some more of those Voyager gold records like we did back in the seventies so that if any aliens are out there they'll be able to see what life was like back on earth. That, for a moment of time in the history of the universe, we played football. I hope NFL Films gets a copy of the Super Bowl in 2017 on one of those records. There won't be another comeback like that, even in five billion more years.

The point is: Stars come and go. They have life cycles. They come into existence, burn for millennia, run out of gas, and then implode. The middle phase, which we are enjoying right now with our sun, is relatively peaceful and reliable, at least from our perspective. Scientists call this part the "main sequence"—fuel is abundant, fusion is ongoing, energy is radiating outward, and the warmth we experience on earth (while fluctuating between, say, Miami in

September and Buffalo in January) is more or less perfect for us as a species to thrive. I like the main sequence.

At some point in your life, if you are lucky enough to experience sustained success, you will become a star. Economists and business-people say that our era of peak performance typically comes in our forties. In football and most athletics, of course, that peak is shifted downward, and many athletes consider their peak to begin later in their twenties, and they try to sustain it for as long as possible.

At some point, they, and you, will no longer be able to sustain it.

Drew Bledsoe was a star. He was a star in college, and he was a star when the Patriots drafted him first overall in 1993. He was tall, stoic, and looked the part. He was the $100 million man who signed a ten-year contract for $103 million in 2001, announced to great fanfare and with smiles all around (including my own). During that time, he came into his "main sequence": he delivered yards, touchdowns, and wins, and he filled up the franchise record book. He took the team to the Super Bowl and in general helped a moribund franchise get back on its feet.

And then he moved into the next phase.

I felt that signs of decline had been there, despite his star power. I had coached against Drew when I was with Cleveland, and I noticed that he was relatively wild when throwing to his left. To me, his perception time—how fast he could see a play unfolding in front of him and make the necessary adjustments to counter what he saw—was also starting to slip. His arm strength was good, but sometimes his capacity to push for the big downfield pass meant that he missed some shorter-yardage plays that keep drives alive.

And then came the horrible injury to Bledsoe during the second game of the 2001 season. Tom stepped in, and we began to rack up wins almost immediately. Bledsoe worked hard, rehabbed responsibly, and competed, but when he was finally cleared to play again, Brady had gone 5–2 as a starter during Bledsoe's recovery. Brady took all the practice snaps while Drew was injured. I was confident that I was making the right choice, and my confidence was quickly rewarded with results. When Drew returned to practice in week ten, prior to our Sunday-night meeting against the Rams in Foxborough, I decided to split the practice plays evenly between Drew and Tom and let them compete for the starting QB position. I felt that Brady practiced better than Bledsoe that week and Brady started against the Rams. Tom struggled in the loss, throwing one TD to two interceptions. I had always known that splitting reps was no way to properly prepare a starting QB for a game, but now it was glaringly obvious. I came to a fork in the road. I had to make a decision about who was going to be the Patriots' starting quarterback, and after making that decision, I was going to give that player all the plays in practice so that he would be adequately prepared to play his best. That was when and why I made the decision to name Tom as the starter. Brady played an outstanding game the following week after taking all the practice snaps, as he threw four TDs and no interceptions.

Drew was upset about my decision, to say the least. It seemed clear to me Drew felt that I'd lied to him and that he was entitled to get his position back. In my opinion, Tom earned the job with his performance, and most important, I felt that Tom gave our team the best chance to win. As the head coach, my responsibility was to the entire team, all fifty-three players, not one individual. Eventually, I think that Drew accepted my decision and Bledsoe helped us beat Pittsburgh in the AFC Championship game when he relieved Brady after Tom injured his ankle in the second quarter. But here's the truth: He was no longer in his main sequence. And we had a new star that needed exposure and room to grow. Tom was winning. Tom was ready to start his main sequence.

The point of this story is not to be critical of Bledsoe. I am telling this to illustrate that, at some point, every leader will have to make a critical and controversial decision. My job was to think of the team first, and my decision to keep Tom as our starter was based on what was best for our football team, and nothing else—regardless of anything that has been said or written elsewhere. Drew played for several more seasons and was selected for another Pro Bowl up in Buffalo. He had a fantastic career and it's a testament to his character and competitiveness that a frustrating final season in New England was followed by a productive last chapter. That's what stars do. Even when they start to diminish, they still burn.

Star players can be burdened by expectations. I recognize this and am sympathetic to it. My prescription is simple: compete, and then compete some more. Never stop competing. I do take some pride in the culture we established within the Patriots even during my first, relatively disappointing season: No one had "tenure." No one owned his job or was *owed* his job. Compete with integrity so that the other players competing for your position can learn from you and take your job one day. If that makes you mad to think about, good.

Drew gave a now-famous locker room interview after learning that, despite being cleared to play, Tom would remain the starting quarterback. "I look forward to getting the chance to compete for my job," he said.

In my opinion, that statement was a step in the right direction. That's what we do in football. We compete with other stars. And not one of us lasts forever.

COMPETITION MAKES EVERYONE RAISE THEIR GAME. SEEK IT OUT. BUT NO ONE PLAYS FOOTBALL FOREVER. MY PHILOSOPHY (BORROWED AND ADAPTED FROM RETIRED REAR ADMIRAL TOM LYNCH) IS TEAM, TEAMMATE, SELF. WHEN I THINK ABOUT WHAT IS

BEST FOR THE ENTIRE TEAM, HARD DECISIONS BECOME CLEAR. DEALING WITH THE INDIVIDUALS AFFECTED BY THE DECISION CAN BE CHALLENGING, BUT THE DECISION ITSELF IS DRIVEN BY WHAT IS BEST FOR THE TEAM.

PREPARATION

There are ways to prepare to win. If there's one thing everyone needs to realize about winning, it's this: the price of success is paid in advance. Good preparation leads to winning—in general, the winner will be the best-prepared team.

I've been a coach and a general manager, but I've also made airport runs and cut game tape. I've done just about every job you can do around the game of football, and each one was a part of the bigger picture. Each one helped me and helped my team. Preparation isn't simply about doing your homework or logging some hours. I've seen plenty of coaches and leaders waste time by holding long meetings for no good reason at all. That's just a performance of preparation, something to get out of the way before the real work begins. Real preparation is a *way* of working, not something that you check off a list.

I've never liked workers who look busy all the time for no good reason. I don't like having too many people. Real preparation involves work that is specifically pointed in a direction, and that direction must add something to the team. When I am looking to promote someone, I can only go by their work and attitude in their current position. "Potential" has become a totally misunderstood word. It doesn't mean there's some kind of secret substance imbued in certain people that helps them get noticed. If it's secret, I don't care about it. I care about your work, and what it says about how you might perform on something more demanding. "Potential" should be a verb.

I tell new players something very similar: Tom Brady wasn't always Tom Brady. When he came into our team, he was a sixth-round draft pick and a fourth-string QB. Rob Gronkowski wasn't always Rob Gronkowski. Edelman caught about fifty total passes in his first couple years. Pat Mahomes sat on the bench for a year. All those players learned, practiced, and prepared for a future when they might be called upon. They were all ready to be great when their greatness was necessary. But they got those opportunities only because they excelled in the small things they were asked to do before they ever could have done anything big. There isn't a workplace in the world that doesn't operate this way. Everyone starts in the mailroom.* And everyone with any kind of power monitors that mailroom to see who's taking their job seriously and who deserves to move up.

Everyone has a choice. A young person can commit to a routine, apply himself to his entry-level job—or he can wake up, check his phone, and go along with whatever his friends have planned that day. One path is preparation; the other isn't anything at all.

As I grew up in my dad's shadow, I observed several ex-Navy

---

* *Almost* everyone, but this book isn't for the people born on third base. They don't need it.

football players work for him as scouts. These military men were truly outstanding and some went on to have exemplary military careers (John Hopkins, Phil Monahan, Terry Murray) and some similarly outstanding coaching careers (George Welsh, Jon Batchelor, Jim Royer). I learned to appreciate these men who worked for my dad—they worked hard, without looking for credit or titles. They only wanted to do their job well so that they would be asked to do more and make a bigger contribution to the Navy football team. Fortunately, my father's assistants also took time to help me and provided examples of how to gain the respect and trust of the boss.

As I embarked on my coaching career, I tried to do the same things I saw from the men who worked for my dad. It was basically simple: do whatever you are asked, and do it as well as you can so that others can do *their* jobs with your preparation work. I learned the importance of assisting coaches so that the position coaches and coordinators could prepare the team.

Of all the things we do to prepare for a football game, the most important is practice. I always try to make practice harder than the game. Unlike sports such as baseball, basketball, and hockey, where there are so many games and opportunities to prepare and improve, football game days are too few, and wins are too precious to experiment with. Game experience is important, but real improvement comes on the practice field, as well as in meetings, walk-throughs, and the weight room.

We drill every situation through repetition and attention to detail. We review every situation over and over. Two-minute offense, goal line defense, backed up in our own end. If it's pouring rain or if the windchill is in the single digits, we rarely move practice to a more comfortable setting. We call it "being comfortable being uncomfortable." We embrace it and work through it, knowing we're eventually going to have to play in those conditions. If the forecast calls for rain on game day, we practice with wet balls—balls doused in water, soap, silicon spray. If we're playing a team with defensive linemen who are especially good at batting down passes, we'll give our scout team linemen paddleball racquets to hold up in the QBs' faces for every pass. (Boy did Tom love this.) To help our corners learn not to grab the opposing player's jersey (and make it easy for the refs to call pass interference), we'll make them wear boxing gloves. No player would honestly claim to enjoy it. It's hard and it's tedious. But you know what? Our best teams were the ones that didn't care how big the game was or how critical the situation was. They *knew* they were prepared, and they were just executing plays they'd done all year long in dress rehearsals. If you demonstrate in practice that you can do something, it gives you confidence you can do it under pressure during competition. Just as important, it gives your teammates confidence that they can trust you. That allows them to perform freely at their job without having to worry about covering for weaker links.

The point I want to get across isn't that you should practice so much that you feel like you're operating on autopilot. You can become brittle and easy to rattle if you think of preparation in those terms. The point is to be consistent. Every game is not the AFC Championship. Every day does not revolve around closing a big deal or scoring a big new client. But those days when the stakes are very high should feel exactly like every other day. Not because you come to work frantic and hyped out of your shoes, but because you approach every day at the office in the same way, and with the same attitude: your preparation today will be your win tomorrow. And if you can reach that level of consistency, you'll have almost unconsciously developed an unshakable confidence. I've seen it happen. When you prepare, you believe.

Coaches can improve in practice just like players. My son Steve relished the chance to call defenses when he was running the scout team against Tom Brady. This experience proved to be valuable when he began to call defenses in games in 2019.

Carl Banks was a player who prepared at an elite level. Honestly, I had trouble keeping up with both Carl and Tom—they were very, very detailed in their preparation. Carl had the best key I have ever seen. When I was defensive coordinator for the Giants, he found a tip on John Spagnola, who played tight end for the Eagles in the mid-eighties. Carl studied the stance of Spagnola and discovered that, incredibly, Spagnola wiggled his fingers on running plays and did not wiggle them on passes. When Banks told me about this, I thought it was a joke. It was not. I looked at all the end zone film and the key held up. I couldn't believe it. After the first series of each game against the Eagles, Carl would come off the field with a big smile, saying, "He's still doing it." Carl had incredible recall and would come into our Tuesday meetings armed with information: stats from every game our opponent had played that year (not to mention previous years) or memory of a play from ten weeks ago that he wanted us to have a game plan for. He also wanted to know about *all* the possibilities we might see in terms of opponent strategy; he wouldn't be satisfied with knowing what they were most likely to do. We needed to be covered there, he would argue. His close attention to detail kept the staff on their toes, and I loved it. He helped me see the game through the eyes of a quarterback, and I helped him see the game through the eyes of a defensive coach. It was a relationship that helped both of us evolve and become more rounded.

SITUATIONAL PREPARATION

Like Carl, Tom Brady was a hard player to coach. I mean that as the highest compliment I can give. Tom forced me to prepare more than normal because I didn't want to be embarrassed by the fact that he studied our opponent's defense more than I did. Around 2005, Tom and I were together in our usual Tuesday-morning meeting. I made a comment like "I haven't seen our opponent play a certain coverage—I don't think they have that adjustment."

Tom let me down easy by saying, "I thought I might have seen that adjustment last year in the Green Bay game."

To be clear, he didn't *think* he saw that coverage adjustment—he absolutely *knew* he saw the adjustment. He was being nice. I was embarrassed. I hadn't prepared as well as Tom. I tried to make sure that I did not make the same mistake again. The bottom line on my meetings with Tom was I didn't want to let him down, and that is the essence of elite preparation.

Even guys like Carl and Tom, however, can't prepare for everything that might happen. We all know you can't prepare for every possibility. You can try, but every once in a while, a cat runs onto the field. The stadium lights go dark for an hour. Or the GPUs you were planning to install in your workstations are 500 percent more expensive than last time you upgraded because someone decided to invent something called Bitcoin. You can't prepare for flukes.

But you can prepare for situations. Football is a game of situations. First and ten. Fourth and one. Down by six with forty seconds to go.

- Offensively, down by four with a minute to go in the game, one time-out, ball at midfield . . .
- Offensively, down by three with twenty-five seconds left in the game, no time-outs, and we're in field goal range . . .
- Defensively, they're at their own one-yard line—what are we ready for?
- Defensively, they need an FG to tie the game. How do we keep them out of FG range?
- Getting out of bounds, keeping them in bounds.

We need a plan for all of these and hundreds more. How do we know we're prepared for these situations that involve everybody? Simple. When everybody *knows what to do*. Everyone needs to know what we are trying to do in key situations. Everyone needs to know, in those situations, how to do their job, because the quarterback or defensive signal caller can't possibly tell everyone in that moment what they should do or be looking for.

How do we all learn what to do? By devoting extra time to cover the situations that determine the outcome of the game and by discussing them, by practicing them. Situations you might encounter a handful of times a year, but which will determine who wins whenever they come up. For instance, if our specialized "hands team" recovers an onside kick at the end of a game, we will almost certainly win.

Falcons fans, you have fair warning. I'm about to talk about 28–3.

Erasing a second-half twenty-five-point deficit means us scoring and keeping them from scoring, over and over. It takes everybody. In most games, you have about five plays of what we call "Got to Have It" (GTHI). That's when everyone in the stadium knows the next play is going to contribute *significantly* toward winning or losing. It's no secret to either team. Our best versus their best. Best play call, best defense, best personnel on the field, best effort.

When you're down twenty-five points in the third quarter, pretty much every play the rest of the way is GTHI territory.

With eight minutes left in the game, we were down two touchdowns and the Falcons had the ball on third and one. If they picked up this one yard, they'd bleed another few minutes off the clock and it would be virtually impossible to come back.

Enter Dont'a Hightower, one of the smartest, toughest, and most clutch players I've ever coached. Instead of merely stopping the Falcons from getting a first down, instead of merely making them punt, Hightower made one of the best and smartest plays I have ever seen. On the previous play, the Atlanta running back Tevin Coleman was injured. The Falcons had carried only two running backs to the game, so Devonta Freeman, the Falcons' early down running back, replaced Coleman. We knew that Freeman was poor at picking up his blitz assignment, so defensive coordinator Matt Patricia and I agreed that a blitz was the right call after Coleman went out of the game.

Hightower was supposed to blitz from the line of scrimmage, but he was lined up off the ball. Actually, I thought he'd missed his assignment. But when Hightower saw Freeman look away, he knew to walk up to the line of scrimmage just before the ball was snapped. Freeman didn't see Hightower approach, and that meant Hightower could blitz past Freeman, who was looking inside, and strip sack QB Matt Ryan in a game-changing play. Talk about being prepared! Hightower took advantage of the substitution and read the next play perfectly. (By the way, that makes *two* Super Bowls in which Dont'a Hightower made a game-changing play that was crucial to the Patriots' victory.)

That's situational awareness. That's preparation.

PREPARING AGAINST THE WELL PREPARED

I'm far from the first person to prioritize preparation. Preparation is not exactly a secret, or anything anyone else hasn't already figured out. (There's a reason that SAT prep is a billion-dollar industry.) But there's a piece to it that I think is underappreciated and underexplored: how to prepare to win when you have limited time and resources.

So far, we have covered how preparation is a way of working rather than some kind of prework, how preparation should be converted one to one into confidence, and how to determine what situations are most important to prepare for. The next level of preparing to win is about how to prepare for . . . other people who prepare.

In any career, you'll eventually reach the point where you can't get ahead just by doing the small stuff well enough. At a certain point you'll need to beat the other guy who wants the job just as badly as you do, or does it just as well (if not better).

Most of the very best players I have coached against prepared at an exceptional level. Peyton Manning, Ray Lewis, Ed Reed—they could walk up to the line of scrimmage, see where one person in a different-color jersey was standing or how he was moving, and know what was coming. They were incredible at it. Some of that comes from natural instincts, but the rest comes from knowing how to study for the test. In order to compete against those guys and beat them, we have to operate at their level by doing two things: be as prepared as them and constantly mix up what we're doing.

Lawrence Taylor, Mike Vrabel, Terry Kinard, Tedy Bruschi, and Rodney Harrison were five of the most instinctive defensive players I coached. They all had an incredible ability to see the game in a special way. At times it seemed like they must have heard the offensive play in the huddle. LT had rare instincts. He could actually tell who was blocking him by how scared they were when they lined up across from him. For instance, if the offensive lineman (or QB) wasn't tense, LT knew it was a run, because the QB didn't have to worry about getting hit. When the QB *was* tense and anxious, LT knew it was a pass. How LT could determine who was tense with such precision, I will never know. He might not be able to explain it either. He just knew.

PUTTING IT ALL TOGETHER

Once you get preparation down, it's time to perform. Preparation creates confidence, builds mental toughness, and helps smart players like Dont'a Hightower have the info they need to do what they do best: win the game. Sometimes that happens because things just swung your way. But when you prepare all week, all year, all your career for something, and you pull it off . . . there's no better feeling in the world.

I have never felt as physically drained coaching a game as I did during the 2004 Super Bowl against the Carolina Panthers. It had everything. Scoring droughts (zero points in the first and third quarters) and scoring deluges (twenty-four points in the second quarter, thirty-seven in the fourth). It was the longest Super Bowl ever played to that point, and being indoors in Houston made for sweltering conditions. The flow of the game was very unusual— twenty penalties is a lot for the Super Bowl—and there were some major injuries and unexpected twists, including something that happened during the halftime show that changed live broadcasts forever (for the younger readers: google "wardrobe malfunction").

Super Bowl preparation produces mountains of information. In the lead-up we had ten-pound binders made, overstuffed with pages upon pages detailing everything that happened in Carolina's previous nineteen games: what they liked to do to start drives, where on the field they took shots at big plays, their favorite trick plays, strengths and weaknesses of every player, blitzes they ran in week four, coverages they ran in their six down-to-the-wire games. It was all useful, and it prepared us for everything that could happen.

Until it didn't.

Defensively, we entered the game hyper-focused on handling offensive coordinator Dan Henning's gap-running scheme that found different ways to "split" the defense. But due to overall game chaos, our focus had to adapt. Looking back, it's almost like we played two or three different games in one game. On Carolina's first six drives, we forced six punts and a fumble. They ran the ball nine times. On their final three possessions, we allowed three touchdowns and they ran the ball only twice. Not exactly how you draw it up.

That was the year we acquired Rodney Harrison, and it didn't take long for him to become a versatile all-world Patriot. He and our other starting safety, Eugene Wilson, had played every game that year, and nearly every play. Their communication, versatility, and playmaking were elite. Along with Ty Law, and cornerbacks Asante Samuel and Tyrone Poole, our secondary was a serious strength.

So when both Harrison and Wilson were injured during the game, we were in serious trouble. We had contingencies for losing one player in a game, but losing two at the same position was a little trickier to manage. The scoring pattern reflected the downgrade in position strength. We weren't stopping anything.

In the span of eight minutes in the fourth quarter, we went from being up eleven to down one.

Then, almost as quickly, we went from being up by seven to being in a tie ball game with a minute left. Thanks to our safeties, it was apparent we weren't going to stop them defensively—but, at the same time, they couldn't cover us. Their line was overwhelming, but our passing game was carving them up. If we could just give Tom a split second longer, he and wide receiver Deion Branch were going to do damage. That's what the game came down to: a classic "last shot" game. We approached our final offensive drive feeling that whoever had the ball last would probably win.

We hadn't prepared to lose our safeties, but we had prepared for something even more significant: that their defensive line would overpower our offensive line. We knew that if our undersized guys could stand up just enough, and buy Tom just enough time, he and our receivers would capitalize. They did. We did. We were mentally tough enough to withstand their awesome line play because we knew it was coming. We prepared. And we won.

I know that I've done a lot here to link preparation and winning, and created the idea that one immediately flows to the other in a simple case of cause and effect. But I'd like to take a step back for a moment and address a logical question that might disrupt that framework.

What about all the preparation that never actually gets utilized? What about all that studying you did . . . and the professor switches things up at the last minute? Does it count? Does it contribute to winning?

If we win a tough game, say, on the last play of the game in a defensive red-zone stand, all the work that we put into red-zone defense that year is retroactively deemed to have been preparation—a direct line can be drawn from A to B. But what if we work equally hard throughout the season, run the same drills, study the same film, and the ball simply doesn't bounce our way in that last play? It's the football equivalent of a tree falling in the forest: Does anyone hear—or, I guess, in this case, see—it?

I'm reminded of an interesting quote from the NBA superstar Giannis Antetokounmpo. He was fresh off a playoffs defeat in a series in which his team was favored to win, and in the press conference following the final game, a reporter asked if he considered the season to have been a failure. Press conferences can be understandably raw experiences for players and coaches (especially when they're following a game that's abruptly ended their season), so it wouldn't have been a surprise if the question was met with an outburst of frustration or defiance or anguish. Instead, Giannis offered something very different:

Do you get a promotion every year at your job? No, right? So every year, your work is a failure? No. Every year, you work toward something, which is a goal: It's to get a promotion, to be able to take care of your family, provide a house for them, or take care of your parents. It's not a failure, it's steps to success. There's always steps to it. Michael Jordan played for fifteen years and won six championships. The other nine years were a failure? That's what you're telling me. There's no failure in sports. There's good days, bad days, some days you are able to be successful, some days you're not, some days it's your turn, some days it's not your turn. That's what sports are about. You don't always win, some other people are gonna win. And this year, someone else is gonna win. Simple as that.

The calm and collected statement surprised a lot of people, as did the rare vulnerability and candidness it displayed. Some, though, thought Giannis was denying the reality in front of him: his team had just lost a series against a team they were supposed to beat, and as the superstar on the team, he owned the largest share of that failure.

I have a slightly different perspective. Were there failures during the game, during the preparation for the game, during the strategizing for the game, that led to the loss? The answers to all are yes. Failure must be addressed, but it's a part of every endeavor, in sports, business, and life. No one bats 1.000. But you've still *lost*. Losing is intolerable.

As I have mentioned throughout this book, wins and losses in life are going to be significantly more ambiguous than they are in football. For us, wins are about points—or, what those in electoral politics call "first past the post"; it doesn't matter if you win the support of 49 percent of the voters if 51 percent support the other guy.

But I agree with Giannis's statement in one respect: the final score does not invalidate the work or commitment that went into getting there in the first place. Preparation—and that's really what we're talking about—is not erased by any final score. A lot of that preparation, if not most of it, represented real work, and real intelligence.

I do not say this in a touchy-feely kind of way—far from it, actually. Preparing hard, working hard, studying hard, and still losing should be something you are unable and unwilling to accept. Instead of feeling good about what you have done, or thinking it's enough (or childishly despairing that "nothing matters" and it's not worth preparing in the first place), you must work even harder. Harder than you even imagined you would have to. A setback is like seeing a brand-new horizon of work that you failed to comprehend could have existed. Now it's time to get there, faster.

Has every year that I've failed to win a Super Bowl been a failure?

Big picture? Maybe not. But I live in my picture. Every loss simply makes me viscerally hate losing more, and every win makes me want to win more. The impact on my will to prepare comes out even and keeps extending forward.

EVERY SITUATION YOU CAN IMAGINE CAN BE PREPARED FOR.

PREPARATION IS NEVER WASTED, REGARDLESS OF OUTCOME.

EIGHT

IMPROVEMENT

There was something different about my father. I could see it whenever I had the opportunity to watch him work. As a scout and coach for the US Naval Academy in Annapolis, his job was to prepare the Navy coaches and players for their next opponent, and to coach players who would fit its unique system and culture—he had been a naval officer and served in Normandy and Okinawa, so he fit right in with the buttoned-up mentality. You just do not waste time in the navy. His work didn't look like other people's work. He didn't mix business with pleasure. While other scouts might mosey around on the sidelines (or by the concessions stand) chatting and gossiping, my father would be taking notes with one of a dozen or so of his immaculately sharpened pencils. No one gets everything right in the talent-spotting game, but if my father missed on a player, it wasn't going to be because he literally missed him. He succeeded at his work for about three decades. His dedication was, and is, legendary.

Coincidentally, my friend Nick had a similar kind of father: demanding of excellence, but quick to reframe a setback as an opportunity for growth. His father and mine both had high expectations for everyone around them, and shared a contagious winning attitude that made those expectations seem possible. Nick has come a long way from his father's business: Saban's Service Station in West Virginia. He's retired now, but I believe he has won a few football games.

I am at a point in my career where I can look back and realize how extraordinary my own father's effort and intensity were, especially because he hadn't always been a scout. He joined the staff at the Naval Academy in 1956, under head coach Eddie Erdelatz, after serving as head coach at a small college in Ohio and as assistant coach at Vanderbilt and North Carolina. At Vanderbilt, the coaches were asked to resurrect a program that hadn't seen sustained success since the old glory days of Dan McGugin (who in the 1910s and '20s had innovated kicking, forward passing, punting, lateral passing, nutrition, and signal-calling, and apparently could be relied on by his players to chip in when they needed to take their girlfriends out for dinner). My father and the rest of the staff were building toward that success when the fickle powers that be at the university decided to clean house. The coaches, including my father, were fired and pushed out.

It was an ugly episode, but it didn't put a dent in his dedication. (I understand, now, how unusual and remarkable that is.) In fact, it didn't change how he worked at all—whatever his thoughts and feelings were about his ouster, the work was the work, and he was going to be the best at whatever came next. It was all an opportunity to grow. He had a passion for improvement. Improvement as a daily practice. Improvement as identity. Improvement as something that simultaneously humbles you (because you know you'll never touch the ceiling of what's possible) at the same time as it dignifies your work, whatever it might be.

Was this part of his personality? Sure. He was a hardworking man his whole life, as his own parents had been. But you don't have to be a Steve Belichick to be that committed. You don't have to join the navy. You certainly don't have to be a football scout. You just have to understand that every time you go to work, you are either building something or wasting your—and your colleagues'—time.

To be clear, the message in this chapter isn't just for those of you who are starting out on your careers or working your way up the ladder. "Improvement" may be misunderstood as a transition or temporary action, a means to an end. Improvement is not "getting ahead"—improvement is working to get better at your job every day. My dad did that well into the sixth decade of his career. Over a whole career, you cannot compartmentalize improvement. Instead, you have to imagine improvement as the medium through which your work should flow. Am I working toward something? Or am I just working? On a football team, we do not have the time to set aside certain days for "improvement." The improvement is inherent in the way we do the daily work, the practices, the film sessions. Everything.

I suspect that the quest for improvement is not quite so ubiquitous in the world outside sports. That's a shame, but it's also why I'm writing this book. Similarly, my father was so committed to improvement he wrote a book—*the* book—on football scouting so that he could help other people improve as well.

But before we can talk improvement, we have to talk about why it matters so much in the first place. It's not mysterious. Most of the time, most of us, in most of what we do, are just not good enough.

I've been there plenty of times.

• • •

You might have heard it said once or twice: "On to Cincinnati." It's a phrase that has made its way into the pantheon of press conference clips, alongside Coach Jim Mora's "Playoffs!?" and Allen Iverson's "Practice . . . ," though that was not my intention on the first day I said it in 2014. I really just was pointing out the fact that our next stop, literally, was Cincinnati; that the game we had just played was in the past and we were now focused on our next opponent. But if you say it fifteen times in about a half hour, like I did that afternoon, you are sending a different message.

We had just taken a 41–14 drubbing at the hands of Kansas City during Monday Night Football, but the score didn't tell the whole story.

The whole story, basically, was that we were terrible, all of us. The head coach, the coordinators, the quarterback, all the other players did not belong in a conversation about good teams. The Chiefs were magnificent. Quarterback Alex Smith finished twenty out of twenty-six with three touchdowns. Their running backs averaged more than five yards per carry. A young tight end by the name of Travis Kelce had a standout game in his first true season. And I was miserable.

Two days later, I didn't have much to say to the media during our midweek press conference. It had been a decade since our last Super Bowl win, and I knew what was coming—more questions about whether we had enough talent, about Tom, about what was going wrong. But my job was not to help the media put together another article on our dysfunction. My job, as I saw it, was to speak to my team. And my message was laser-focused on improvement.

The New England Patriots were expected to win, and sometimes we didn't. That's football. But we were certainly not expected to get *crushed*. We had future Hall of Famers, current Pro Bowlers, and plenty of champions, and still we were 2–2 on the season, coming off one of the worst losses I could remember. But it was October, and there was time. It wouldn't be enough to "return to form" or to get back to playing how we normally did. We needed to be better because we could be better. My fixation on Cincinnati was just a way to tell my players and coaches: what happens next is up to us.

My players understood. The other coaches understood.

Improve. Do nothing else. Just improve.

How do you avoid getting stuck after a big loss? How do you keep hope for improvement alive when everything's collapsed and your whole plan has failed? You sometimes see a football player after he makes a mistake put his hands up around his head and bend over so that he's curled up, almost like he's hiding. This is anti-improvement. It's myopic. At a moment when he should be thinking about what he can do next for his team, he's stuck in his own head replaying his own failure.

I'm not good enough is a thought that creeps in when you get too caught up in a setback. It's what many people feel when they get fired like my father did. *If I was better*, you think, *they couldn't have fired me*. This is an attitude that chokes off the possibility of improvement. "If I was better" means that you don't think you can be. It keeps you in a losing mentality. I can understand the feeling of wanting to punish yourself, but the reality is there's no time. There's no time in a football game for personal journeys into the psyche. Go drink some Gatorade and grab a tablet to review the play. It's time to improve.

The first thing you need to do is to create space by keeping focused on what ultimately matters. Improvement is a time-saver and a time organizer. The week of practice that followed the disastrous Kansas City game was extraordinarily effective. When I set the agenda—"On to Cincinnati"—it immediately clarified what work we needed to do. There was no time for dwelling on mistakes (there were too many to dwell on anyway) or being defensive about who'd done this, who'd done that, who was responsible for that busted play, and who actually did an adequate job. Here's what there was time for: accountability and taking ownership over lapses that could not happen again. If you think you're committed to improvement but you're still fooling around during the day and wasting time at work, you are lying. You're paying lip service to what really matters.

When things are not going well, or you want to be in a better position, I have three pieces of advice: (1) Do not blame anyone or make excuses, (2) Understand what you need to do to improve the situation, and (3) Take positive steps to affect change.

Excuses do not make your situation any better. Blaming others might make you feel better, but won't make any difference. What actually will help is improvement, and improvement involves two basic steps: identifying what needs to change and taking action to change it. Improvement is as simple as it sounds. Find out what you need to do and do it.

INSPIRING IMPROVEMENT

When there are too many things going the wrong way, and too many players doing the wrong things, they need to be told directly to make the commitment they were hired to make. There needs to be a communication, to everyone, about where we stand.

After our loss to the Chiefs, I could have gone up in that press conference and called out players, coaches, and my own mistakes. I could have named names. (There is a time for that, but that wasn't it.) Instead, I just said one thing: "On to Cincinnati." Three words, one big signal. We were still in this, and I didn't need to look back. My commitment was to using my clock wisely.

On bad teams, you have time. If we were 2–2 and we didn't have the talent to finish above .500, maybe I would have gotten more granular about where we had failed, where I had failed, where our players had failed to execute. Bad teams improve at a slower rate. But in 2014 we didn't have time. We were a good team, and I knew it. The rest of the team just had to know it too.

That's what team film sessions are for. I must have said it a hundred times a day in front of the screen: "Here's what I'm talking about . . ." It wasn't to embarrass anyone or call them out. It was to hold them accountable, and to hold us coaches accountable for failing to have fixed a problem during a game. Some people from outside the organization thought these sessions were devastating for players and ground down their confidence. That couldn't have been less true. There was no time for me to put on some big dog-and-pony show and yell about this or that until I was red-faced. We pointed out errors. The effects were positive. Sure, there were some bad feelings, but they were temporary—and the idea was to channel them toward correction, toward the goal, toward Cincinnati, and not back toward the player himself. No one got to mope.

We avoid unproductive nit-picking by not getting into "why" when we look at our mistakes. Unless it's part of a chronic problem, I don't care much about why that guard moved a split second too early and got us a penalty. I care about what *to* do and what *not* to do (and I have been, over the years, producer, director, and narrator of thousands of "How Not to Do It" videos). Focus on what you can see, not on gathering circumstantial evidence. We all make mistakes. Just don't make them repeatedly.

My job is to point out those mistakes without the players feeling like I am blaming them and understanding instead that I am doing my job as a coach, so that we can make the right adjustment in the future and execute the play better. My job is to get the play right, and that cannot happen unless everyone knows what went wrong.

IMPROVING YOURSELF

What was the first task you were asked to do at your job? Answer a phone? Write an email? Fetch some coffee? Open up Excel and clean up the mess the last guy left? I bet it wasn't all that exciting, and probably not all that rewarding. I also bet you messed it up, at least a little bit.

Chances are you have progressed since then. Maybe you've been promoted, or maybe you went back to school, got a degree, got a new job. Now you look around and see people just starting out, like you did, and they're doing the same things you were doing: the unexciting but essential tasks that keep the workplace humming along and healthy. And now you can see what you couldn't see back then: the difference in how people do even the smallest of things. Now, standing where you are, you can tell the difference between someone just logging hours and someone who's actually engaged with the work, however tedious, and executing it with an interest in getting better. People who want to improve listen to instructions, work efficiently, and immediately own up to mistakes in the spirit of course correction. People who want to improve take the initiative whenever they might have it, however rare, and if they're asked to do the same thing every day, they find ways to do it better and faster. I can't promise that every job will be fun, but people who want to improve have more fun because there are aspects of their jobs that can resemble games. They challenge themselves. They get creative. They find ways to make the tedious parts of their jobs as automatic as possible. Improvers stand out, even before their job performance actually improves. You did, once. Now you can spot it.

The process is continuous. It's not a moment of evaluation once a year, and it's not some therapeutic exercise in which you write down your goals and make little check marks. That's summer camp stuff. Improvement is a mindset you apply to whatever work you have in front of you, and it either helps you pour yourself into it or makes you realize you aren't ready yet.

My father never stopped improving, and never stopped being appreciated for it. Thanks to his legacy, and his book, he'll be remembered for his virtues and intelligence for a very long time. I never want to stop learning, especially about football.

Improvement might not make you popular. I bet you know what I mean. You're familiar with jealousy, but it goes deeper than that. People who believe in improvement are often preparing or practicing during times when others are not; that difference in commitment can be conspicuous, and threatening. I know this firsthand—because of my belief that improvement is a constant, continuous thing, and must be part of your work in every moment, I was accused once of poor sportsmanship.

It was 2007. We were dominating, but a game against Washington that year was a particularly distinct blowout. Washington's head coach was the legendary Joe Gibbs, a three-time Super Bowl winner in the eighties who had been enticed out of retirement in 2004 to try to lead the team back to glory. He made the playoffs twice during his second time around, but on this day his team was outmatched. We scored the first fifty-two points, which had happened in the NFL only four times since 1980. And then we just kept going. Just because we were winning didn't mean I eased up. At that point, the game wasn't about winning anymore. It was about our habits, our mentality, and our capacity to play a full sixty-minute game without getting gassed. The previous seasons had seen us let up in critical late-game situations, especially in the playoffs, and I was sick of it. So were the players. We would never again be selective about when it was time to compete and when it wasn't. Competition, like improvement, isn't about one quarter, one half, one game, or one season. If it is, you're just setting a date on the calendar when you're apparently comfortable with losing.

After the game, I was initially surprised to hear that the talk around the league and in the media was not about our team's impressive performance but about my "running up the score" on Washington and "poor Joe Gibbs."* My dad taught me something a long time ago and Coach Parcells reinforced it multiple times: As a defensive coach, it is your job to keep the score down, not theirs. If you want to keep the score down, play better defense. I never forgot those words.

Besides, when you commit to improvement, sometimes the game isn't about the opponent at all. Sometimes it's not even about the bottom line in any given day or year. It's about what you need to do in order to be better next time.

And there was going to be a next time. The very next week, in fact, was going to be the toughest and most important game of the regular season: on the road against our biggest rival, the defending Super Bowl Colts. We were 8–0 and they were 7–0. The game was

---

* Besides, fifteen years earlier, Joe Gibbs and his team poured it on in a fourth-quarter blowout against me during my first year as the head coach of the Cleveland Browns. We were bad and they were good, and they deserved to win 42–17 as they did. You might need to locate a microfiche machine to look it up, but try finding anyone talking about "poor Bill Belichick." Didn't happen.

an instant classic. It was well played on both sides of the ball and we had Hall of Famers all over the field. But, offensively, the game was a struggle for us through three quarters. We were down, 20–10, in the fourth when I shouted to a group of players.

"Sixty minutes—you understand me?!" I was loud enough that apparently it's audible in the NFL Films record of the game. Maybe my comment was aggressive or intense or "unsportsmanlike." But it worked. We scored 14 unanswered, forced Peyton into a turnover, and won, 24–20. It was one of the best regular-season performances of any team in my career.

I want to tell you about two special players from New England. One was, and is, a superstar. One is less famous, but was just as integral to a championship. Both improved in outstanding ways during their careers with us.

From the day I got to the Patriots, we always had a pass-catching running back in our offense. This player was as important as anyone else when it came to the overall functioning of the offense, and to Tom in particular. He loved playing with those guys, and he needed them.

It's critical to understand that most defenses that played against Tom Brady knew they were in for a long day. The only teams that had a chance against him were the ones who understood they had to mix things up and try to surprise him. Show a blitz and then don't. Or blitz players from unexpected places. This meant that one of the most important players on the field for us on passing plays was our running back. He was the last line of defense before a blitzing defender could get to Tom.

Looking at James White—five ten, barely two hundred pounds—you wouldn't say, "This is the guy we want protecting the franchise," mainly because it wasn't something that he'd ever been asked to do before. But we saw traits in James that gave us confidence we could work with him. No running back was more diligent or accountable in protection than James White. However complex the defense, James knew who to look out for—and knew how to get in his way.

We drafted him in the fourth round in 2014, a few months after losing to Peyton Manning's Denver Broncos in the AFC Championship game. He was a small runner, and while he had been productive enough back on the ground at Wisconsin, receiving hadn't been a big part of the Badgers' offensive game plan. You may be surprised that someone without any elite physical traits could be the best at anything in a professional sport, but James proved that to be possible. He wasn't big, he wasn't fast, and he had relatively small hands. But he had elite personal traits. His character was the best we could have ever asked for—unselfish, tough, rarely hurt. He knew what he needed to do to transform himself into the type of player we could use, and he worked his butt off to do it. I don't think I've ever coached someone who worked harder or who paid more attention to the people in front of him. He was a sponge. He listened to *every single thing* that was said in meeting rooms and during every drill. He thought about the game like a coach trying to see the entire field.

As a receiver, James learned how to set up defenders, how to come back to the ball when it was in the air. As a blocker he learned how to read defenses. As a runner, he learned how to make people miss. He wasn't an elite runner, but he was good at everything we asked him to do, and that itself is an elite characteristic. It does not come easy, and it is not common. It takes mental fortitude, and it takes elite character. The kind of person who can be honest about what his skills really are, and confident enough in his gifts that he can accept multiple roles. Development is a two-way street. The coach and the player. The teacher and the student. Coaches can instruct, talk, meet, do drills, watch tape until our eyes are bleary. But someone on the other end has to work in concert with us to create the improvement—and work more to make it stick.

Despite his enthusiasm and dedication, James played in only three games his rookie year—barely at all. He was not a factor in the Super Bowl win. And by training camp of the following season, we had long discussions about where he would fit moving forward. It took him a year and a half to establish a role for himself. He was patient, and he was confident in what he had to offer, and he trusted that our system would allow him to show what he could do. He didn't play a role against the Seattle Seahawks in the 2015 Super Bowl, but fast-forward two years, to arguably the most memorable Super Bowl of all, and there he was when it mattered and when we needed him. After all the learning, grinding, working. After mastering several different skills and maxing out his potential. Against Atlanta, against all odds, he got sixteen targets, fourteen receptions, and a walk-off championship TD. Good work for a small running back without skills.

Then there was Rob Gronkowski. He was all motor. He worked hard, he played hard, he practiced hard. In my mind, he embodies the simplest improvement concept: absolutely 100 percent go-go-go *work*. I hesitate to use the phrase "work ethic" when talking about Gronk, but that's only because I think his desire to work is rooted deeper than ethics. It's not a conscious choice. It's innate. I don't think he's ever been any other way.

(Here's a free motivation trick: Whenever you feel lazy, close your eyes and imagine Gronk walking into your office and swatting you aside and taking your job. What's he doing? How hard is he doing it? Does he seem depressed to be working hard? Or did he just spike your coffee mug on your head after sending that email you were too overwhelmed to type?)

Gronk isn't a perfect model for improvement because Gronk is one of a kind. Whatever fire burns within Gronk is something that is not necessarily known to science. Lawrence Taylor is a rare, rare human being. Gronk is an alien.

I'm not sure I ever coached anyone who got more out of his body. Yes, he is six foot six and built like a Terminator. But big bodies can, paradoxically, be a little fragile. It's the same in the NBA, where centers can be dominating, but are relatively quick to accrue injuries, especially to their lower bodies. Gronk was the size of a power forward, but instead of jogging up and down a court he was sprinting—and suddenly stopping—and sprinting again—all over a field, trying to dodge close to a dozen men gunning for his back, his knees, his neck, or whatever might bring his body crashing down to the turf. He was magnificent.

And he built himself into becoming that.

We were able to grab Gronk in the second round in 2010 because he'd just come off a full year of inactivity due to back injuries at Arizona. He was a physical monster, so it was a bet on the idea that he would rehab well, commit himself to getting back into playing shape, and be ready to join up with a team that had perennial championship aspirations. Watching Gronk play at Arizona was actually less than spectacular. He was a good blocker and an average receiver without a lot of opportunities in the passing game. And then his predraft visit to the Patriots facility was one of the worst we ever had—he slept on the floor in the waiting room. He was tired and didn't seem interested in the draft process. My turning point on Gronk was a conversation I had with Arizona Head Coach Mike Stoops. Mike told me that Rob was the hardest worker and toughest player he'd coached. He raved about Rob's hands, based on practice observations, since his receiving opportunities at Arizona were limited. Everything made sense to me: he *could* be great, but Rob had a long, long way to go!

For Gronk, improvement was inevitable. He wanted to work, and he wanted to win. Another thing Mike Stoops told me during the draft was that "All he cares about is winning." He was right. As a testament to that fact, when I eventually tried to trade Rob to the Detroit Lions near the end of his career in 2018, he told me that instead of permitting the trade to a team that would finish fourth in their division he would rather retire. The trade fell through. We won another Super Bowl that year. And Gronk would win another yet, four years after that.

Like winning, improvement is not a goal. It's a practice. Few of us can aspire to improve in the way that Gronk did, as a man of pure motor, or as James White did, as a man of discipline. But we can appreciate how someone can only truly exploit those gifts if he has a force of will—and a commitment to victory—to match. If Lawrence Taylor showed us that someone with extraordinary gifts can succeed despite frequently poor decision-making, Gronk showed us that someone blessed with similar gifts can joyfully improve upon those gifts—and become a legend.

IMPROVEMENT IS CONTINUOUS. IMPROVEMENT REQUIRES HONESTY ABOUT YOUR CURRENT STATUS AND YOUR POTENTIAL. DON'T IMPROVE IN JUST ONE DIMENSION. THE MOST

IMPRESSIVE DEVELOPMENT IS WELL-ROUNDED. THE MORE TALENTS YOU POSSESS, THE MORE USEFUL YOU WILL BE IN ANY KIND OF COMPETITIVE ENVIRONMENT.

NINE

MOVING ON

As a football coach, coming to work the day after a win is a great feeling. Victories in the NFL are hard to achieve. There are no easy wins. The day after a loss is another story, regardless of the circumstances that contributed to defeat. In terms of providing leadership, moving on from a win is usually easy. Helping a team move on after a loss isn't nearly as simple, but the head coach must do it.

If you talk to Patriots fans, most aren't eager to get into 2008. During our very first game, Tom was hit in his left leg by Chiefs safety Bernard Pollard and ended up tearing his ACL and MCL. We hung on to win that game—and won ten more, to get to 11–5—but Tom was sidelined the entire season, and although in many respects we played well and outperformed expectations with Matt Cassel in for Tom, we missed the playoffs during a highly competitive season in the AFC. We spent the postseason at home, just a year after an undefeated regular season had ended with a crushing loss in the Super Bowl.

It was tough. But in September 2009, we were ready to bounce back.

Prior to the start of that season, I agreed to do something no other coach in American professional sports history had ever done: wear a microphone for every game. It was for a documentary called *A Football Life*, and over the course of the season, hundreds of hours of real-time audio was recorded: play calls, conversations with players, arguments, everything. All the emotion and drama of a football season, unrehearsed and uncensored. After the producers listened to this audio, they told me that one moment above all else struck them the most.

A moment of silence, of nothing at all.

It was August 28, 2009, the night of our third preseason game, which is traditionally when starting players play the longest before being subbed out. Everyone's a little on edge already, hoping for two more quarters or so of injury-free football before we get to the homestretch—just stay out of harm's way and let the less-established players come in and get some reps.

Late in the first half, Tom Brady was very much directly in harm's way. He absorbed what was possibly the hardest hit of his entire career, courtesy of Washington's Albert Haynesworth, a defensive tackle and one of the fiercest players in the league. He drilled Tom into the ground, and I fully believe if they had measured the impact force of the hit it would have been right up there with the hit from Pollard that had blown out his knee 355 days earlier.

Déjà vu. A third consecutive season of miserable luck.

After Tom received a brief sideline medical examination, I was informed that Tom had a sore shoulder and was out of the game. This was the moment the documentary producers were waiting for—to see the coach crumble as he received the worst possible news, at the worst possible time, wearing a microphone that he had been dumb enough to agree to wear. . . . What were they going to get? How many bleeps would they have to drop in to make it a family-friendly movie? It might have been hell for me, but it would be good TV, right?

I gave them nothing. But the silence wasn't intentional. I wasn't controlling myself or trying to prove a point. It certainly wasn't because I didn't care. I did care. A lot.

There's no way, really, to prepare for something as devastating as losing your starting QB. You do everything you can to help the backups stay ready, but your starter's talent and know-how is literally irreplaceable. The entire season changes in an instant. And even as we take precautions, get physically prepared, and monitor our health, injuries happen. What does a head coach do when a key player is injured?

As the team leader, a head coach doesn't dwell on a bad break, injury, or some other setback. Life in football, just like life in the military, goes on and the team has to move on, regardless of the circumstances. There are only two reasons people dwell on a bad break, and both are stupid and useless. The first is so you can spend some quality time in a private pity party ("Why me!?"), and the second is because you need some time to lie to yourself about what you just saw. Neither is justifiable. They don't do anything, and they suck your time and attention away from what really matters: what comes next.

Players and assistant coaches generally take their cues on processing a loss from the head coach or their direct supervisor. A good position coach will try to help his position group move on with specific points to his players. When I was an assistant coach, I followed the lead provided by Coach Parcells. I tried to accent Parcells's theme to the defensive staff and players by taking his points and putting them into my own words and by citing specific examples of how our group needed to respond. Support from the head coach is critical because the message gets reinforced to the staff and players. Everyone on defense understood that Parcells's message was heard and that everyone was committed to carrying out his orders. As a head coach myself, I was lucky to have some of the game's best coaches on my staff. Leadership from the coaching staff and key players provides the backbone for the team's ability to move on.

If your player gets injured, thinking about the next play means thinking about what the backup player can do, what he does best, what his strengths and weaknesses are, and how he fits into the plays you practiced that week. In life, that almost always means making the next decision. When you do push on, you aren't necessarily guaranteeing success moving forward—you could, after all, make another mistake—but the only way to guarantee failure is by failing to make any decision at all. "Next play," "next day," "next game" are all appropriate phrases in these moments, but one that always stuck with me was something that Carl Banks would frequently say on the practice field. "Don't let a bad play become a bad day!" I loved that because it captured the moment on the field.

Ray Dalio, the legendary investor and founder of the largest hedge fund in the world, has written about the satisfaction and positivity that can come from radically accepting the results of your decisions, good or bad—or as he puts it, being a hyperrealist: "Just as long-distance runners push through pain to experience the pleasure of 'runner's high,' I have largely gotten past the pain of my mistake making and instead enjoy the pleasure that comes with learning from it," he says.

I cannot claim to have reached this deeply into my own psyche— I still hate losing more than anything—but I understand what he means, and I believe that being realistic does indeed put you in a position to make better decisions. Eventually, the odds will be on your side. I've met plenty of coaches and players who have an easy time "being real" when it comes to sharing their critical appraisal of other people's work, but at some point, you also have to turn that realism on yourself.

I know that Dalio has been a practitioner of transcendental meditation for many years. (Perhaps that's why he gets "mistake learner's high" and I just get pissed off.) That's his moment of inner realism. Mine is another kind of meditation, and during that preseason game against Washington, that's where I was: in the silence. The producers must have been disappointed they didn't get something more explosive—I've done enough television to know that, typically, they're not looking for dead air and quiet contemplation. But anyone who watches that moment knows what's going on. They are seeing what it looks like to be thinking about the next play. A few moments of inner peace . . . perhaps wondering whether trading Matt Cassel in the offseason had been wise. Football meditation.

It turned out that Tom was fine. He would go on to win the NFL Comeback Player of the Year award. Injuries are tough, very tough, on everyone involved with the team. But the team still has to come first. And injuries can be overcome: Kurt Warner replacing Trent Green as QB for the Rams in 1999 and Brady replacing Bledsoe in 2001 are both examples of teams that lost their starting quarterbacks and went on to win Super Bowls. In 2009, the Patriots lost in the playoffs to the Ravens, and we turned our attention to the next season.

This chapter is a little different from the others. All the principles in this book are applicable to anyone at any stage, but in my experience, the wisdom of "the next play" is mostly lost on two kinds of people—or, rather, people in two different stages of life. Those are the guys who are just starting out and the "oldheads" like me who have seen some (or a lot of) success. I'll explain.

New Orleans is one of my favorite places. The energy, people, culture, music, food, history, Southern vibe . . . I love it all. It has an identity and personality that a lot of other places have lost over the years. My first trip to New Orleans came when I was in college. I've been there dozens of times since as a coach, but half a century ago I was just a civilian as I strolled under the balconies and let the trombones and clarinets wash over me in the humid night air. Jim Royer, who was a terrific offensive lineman for Navy's 1954 Sugar Bowl champion team, worked as an assistant for my dad, and they developed a close relationship. I also became close with Jim, who coached at Navy and Tulane before joining with the Archie Manning–led Saints in the early seventies. I would say that my relationship with Jim provided my first adult connection with the NFL. Jim and I talked about coaching and scouting in the NFL and I started to accumulate some pro football knowledge "by osmosis" (as Parcells liked to say).

It was during this time, when I was going to college at Wesleyan, that my fraternity brothers and I road-tripped the fifteen hundred miles from Middletown, Connecticut, to the Big Easy. Four times. Even back then—especially back then—New Orleans was more fun than Middletown.

And what did a bunch of Chi Psi fraternity brothers do for a few days of liberty away from the cold Connecticut winter (and campus restrictions)? We became the fastest regulars in the history of Pat O'Brien's bar, savoring everything we could without a thought for the next day. I don't regret it because for 99 percent of the rest of my life, I've done things completely different. Shortly after Pat

O'Brien's, cross-country frat trips gave way to the more disciplined, demanding (and effective) office of the Baltimore Colts. I made the transition because I knew what to expect. I knew about football from my father and from guys like Jim who did more than just introduce me to New Orleans nightlife.

This is why I make it my duty to tell young people that the time is now to start thinking about tomorrow. That was the advice that was given to me—not in so many words, but in the expectations of the people around me, especially those who had the power to make or break my career. Not everyone has that. College is done. Campus life is over. Pat O'Brien's is closed (metaphorically). There's nothing wrong with savoring life and seeking out good times with the boys. But to bank those days, to provide for them, to ever have a chance of throwing down your card and picking up the tab, you need to start producing at your job. For me, that meant taking advantage of every opportunity. Whatever your work is, you learn from the bottom up, not the top down.

That's as true in football as anywhere else. In 1975 I wrote to 125 football programs about getting a graduate assistant position. I received fewer than 10 replies.* Eventually, Lou Holtz gave me a GA position at NC State and I was accepted to their school of economics in May 1975. One month later, the rules known collectively as Title IX came into effect and NC State awarded all the GA positions to women. I never worked a day there. Lou Holtz was the first coach to hire me and the first coach to fire me. When Ted Marchibroda

---

* As an NFL head coach, I tried to reply to every job application and résumé. I am not saying I got to all of them, but I tried and I wrote back to hundreds of applicants. I don't think things have changed much in the last fifty years because I often get a letter back from the applicant thanking me for being one of the replies, if not the only reply, he received. I think every applicant deserves at least a form-letter response. The few that I received meant a lot to me.

offered me a nonpaying, part-time position with the Baltimore Colts in June 1975, I jumped at the opportunity. I asked him if I could be full-time for the same pay ($0), and he went along with that. My job with the Colts was, literally, everything and anything. I was a ball boy (I snapped the ball to Bert Jones more times than anyone on the team except for Ken Mendenhall, the starting center), and because Coach Marchibroda always wanted Bert to have a center for every passing drill, I got to step in and play that role during drills. It was one of the best jobs I ever had, because for one season I got to hear every word that Coach Marchibroda told Bert in those drills and in the process got a graduate-level tutorial in QB coaching. I also shagged balls for the kicker, Toni Linhart, and I helped prepare play cards for the various coaching staffs. I worked in the equipment room and made copies of scouting reports with our secretary, Maureen. I spent hours traveling to and from the Baltimore airport to ship (or receive) film, and I chauffeured coaches around from Howard Johnson's every day during the regular season. I tried to learn as much as I could about every part of the process and every part of the organization.

The experience of understanding the working process of a football organization was a gift. I did not fully realize the value of my experience until I became a head coach and began to assemble my own staff. Most applicants I talk to don't embrace the concept of understanding how "everything works." They are focused on their chosen career path (for example: QB coach to offensive coordinator to head coach). My first eight years in the NFL essentially consisted of being a graduate assistant for four years and a special teams coach for another four, mixed in with some position coaching responsibility (TE, WR, LB). Ultimately, these diverse experiences gave me a foundation for leading an organization. Coaching defense for Bill Parcells was another level of learning for me, built on the foundation of those first eight years.

. . .

Youth isn't the only time you can get flat-footed and forget to keep looking forward. The other is when you get, well, like me. I've done my share of winning, but it's not enough. Getting "used to" winning is the quickest way for it to stop—it's just as much a barrier to continued success as is dwelling on failures. Whatever mind game you have to play with yourself to get motivated after a big win at work, do it. Celebrate with your team, and then move on. We formalized this at the Patriots organization by assigning a hallway in Gillette Stadium to be our weekly photo gallery (but only after wins). After each win, we would get twenty-five twenty-by-thirty-inch glossy action shots of players making great plays printed and mounted. By the end of the season, there'd be hundreds of them. The photos were a big deal. Players and coaches knew which walls would get the new batch, and they'd flock around to see who made the cut, if their great catch or tackle or interception would be up there in front of everyone. They'd count up their photos as the weeks went on and compare tallies with their teammates. They'd organize as units around reactions—"Why aren't there more offensive linemen up there?"—and lobby to get more photos made. Maybe it surprises you that pro athletes would be dialed into something like that, which any high school coach could just as easily implement. Well, they are. We all are.

Another simple way to kick-start the "next play" mentality: a calendar. I'm serious. Here's the truth about your time when you're a junior employee, or somewhere in the middle of your career: the people who run the place don't think your time is particularly important. (Actually, if they're great leaders and winners, they'll know that it's important, but not necessarily for the same reasons as you might.) It's hard to stay focused on the next play when your day is liable to be interrupted at any moment by a manager or team leader telling you that you need to crash this or that particular project, or, even worse, run out and pick up a present for their spouse's birthday (which you reminded them of).

That's the nature of a hierarchy. Some people call the shots, and even if they're judicious and as fair as possible, their wishes override yours.

Look beyond this reality. Remember that your time is at least partially yours to spend, and make it easier on yourself by creating a schedule. None of us has the brainpower to go into each workday and improvise a good, efficient use of our time—it takes too much attention and energy to weigh possibilities, make calls about effectiveness, and think about which projects we need to push forward on any given day. By the time you come up with a plan for the day, it's lunchtime.

Football is very good for separating the day up into a sequence of decision points: run play, call play, run play, call play, etc. In your workplace, you can emulate this by using a calendar and sticking to it. Make a calendar for your week on Sunday, before the week begins. Fill your days. Be realistic, but be rigid. Don't schedule "free time" (trust that your deep human instinct to goof off will find a way; it always does), and don't make anything general or generic. Plan on Sunday, execute Monday through Friday. The calendar will automate what the "next play" will be and when it will begin.

When your schedule inevitably gets disrupted, you'll feel the pain. And it'll make you want to get back to it as soon as possible. You'll be charged up to get done with the distraction or the urgent project your boss has just dropped on your plate and get back to what you had planned. I can tell you what I'm doing, and thinking, every day for an entire year. Evaluations of our team, schemes, coaches, practices, schedules, processes . . . on down to free-agent decisions, draft preparation, spring practices, opponent study, training camp, and so on. If something else falls through or I am more efficient than I expected, I always have something else I can add to the calendar just in case. By always focusing on what comes next, I naturally put myself in a position to do more, period.

I love dogs. Dogs, like transcendental meditation, have something to tell us about how to face a contradiction that you might be picking up on in this chapter: How are we supposed to focus on what comes next if we're always occupied with it? Thinking about the next play—what to run, who to rely on—requires constant consideration of what's been happening on the field. Doesn't that require exactly the kind of split focus that I'm arguing against?

No. Well, yes. It's the manner of focus that matters. Transcendental meditation probably has an answer for how to both be in the moment and be outside the moment, but so do dogs. Dogs like to take naps, particularly in sunny spots in the house. The challenge is, the sun moves throughout the day—but dogs don't know that. Their focus isn't on how or why it moves, but the simple fact that it feels nice when they line up with it. In the early morning, there's a patch in the kitchen; by midday, that patch has diminished and now the sun is streaming through the big window in the living room. If you watch, you'll eventually see a dog stand up, stretch, and move from the now shady kitchen to the sunny living room. And that's where the second nap of the morning begins. The key here is that he has inseparably attached his focus to his goal. The goal is to take a nap in the sun. The next play is therefore always vividly clear: when the sunny spot moves, move with it.

Call this instinctive goal orientation. No wasted movement, no wasted focus. Instinct negotiates between the dog's goals and the

BILL PARCELLS

Bill Parcells won 172 regular season games as a head coach in the NFL for four different organizations, so page 172 is reserved for him.

I first met Bill when I was with my dad on a scouting trip to West Point in 1967. Bill was the linebacker coach at Army. My dad developed a friendship with Bill in the sixties that grew much closer during the eighties when I worked with Bill at the New York Giants. There was enormous mutual respect between these two great men. Bill was generous with his time and was often like a father to me. He taught me his principles of defensive football. He built the Giants, the Patriots, the Jets, and the Cowboys.

In 2021 before a preseason game, I took the team on a trip to visit NFL Films. Executive producer Ken Rodgers opened up the enormous NFL Films vault and put together some of the highlights and outtakes from a documentary film he had directed a few years earlier about Bill Parcells and me. The team watched about ten minutes of the other Bill yelling at me, cursing me for bad defensive calls, and generally ripping me for a variety of mistakes—and they absolutely loved it. We won the game.

Bill was a great coach, a great mentor for me, and a great friend. He showed confidence and trust in me, and he saw a future for me that I didn't see in myself. I followed about 90 percent of the advice Bill gave me (and I probably would have been better off if I'd followed the other 10 percent too).

If my players and coaches learned anything from me, they should thank you, Bill. Nobody taught me more about coaching in the NFL than you did.

Thanks, Bill. From all of us.

dog's actions. Unfortunately, we humans are not as instinctual as dogs, and we end up letting in a lot of noise and distraction in between our goals and our actions. Fixation on the "next play" is a way of forcing yourself into a goal-oriented stance, and this, in turn, should naturally limit your focus.

I'll give you an example. If I were fixated on "playing correct football"—whatever that might mean—I would have called a time-out before the Seahawks ran their last play of the Super Bowl in 2015. The Seahawks had the ball and twenty-six seconds left in the game. They were behind by four points and it was second down. Either they would score a touchdown and win the Super Bowl, or we would stop them and we would win. The math was clear, and the math would be identical today if two teams ended up in the same situation.

If my goal was to not be wrong, I would have called a time-out. But that was not my goal (and never will be my goal). My goal was to beat the Seattle Seahawks and win the championship. That goal was unwavering, and, as a result, my focus was not on mathematics or on my reputation but on something closer: the sideline of the Seattle Seahawks. What I saw across the field gave me everything I needed to know to decide on my next play, which, in that moment, was not to make a time-out call but to challenge the Seahawks to execute the right play against our goal-line defense. I never want to see the offense run the ball into our end zone. I would rather make them execute a pass play from the one- or two-yard line. Therefore, as the ball approaches our goal line, I try to increase our run defense. By the situation book, I should have called a time-out to save time for us if Seattle scored. But when I looked across the field at the Seahawks' team, something just didn't look right, so I decided to let things play out.

Leading up to that moment, I did not have to divide my focus between any number of conflicting goals and questions, and because of that, my focus automatically narrowed in on what was directly in front of me. All that really mattered were the next several seconds and how they would unfold.

Trust that you can subordinate your focus, if first you subordinate yourself to your goal: doing your job to help the team win.

Ray Dalio talks a lot about being goal-oriented. So much so that he has a five-step process he calls "Do What You Set Out to Do." It's good stuff, but my process eliminates the three middle steps and cuts to the chase. Football craves efficiency.

1. Work for goals that you and your organization are excited about.
2. Cut.
3. Cut.
4. Cut.
5. Ring the bell. (Or, in our case, award game balls to each victory's standout players.)

I like his last step a lot: "ring the bell," or, very simply, register the win. Acknowledge it and let everyone within earshot know about it. It suggests a moment of pause and a moment of celebration.*

But doesn't that clash with my direction to keep moving forward, keep the focus on the next win and not the last?

It does, but only because the secret function of "ring the bell" is the fact that it gets the job done quickly. Just like a whistle cuts

---

* I am sure that my appreciation for this ritual comes subconsciously from my experience as a kid. Navy has a great tradition: when the Navy football team arrives back on campus after beating Army, they assemble at the bell from the *Enterprise* and each player rings it for the number of points by which Navy won. When Navy defeated Army in five straight games from 1959 to 1963, the bell-ringing ceremony was the finale of the weekend.

through the commotion of a football practice and makes it so we coaches don't have to go around to each unit individually and ask for their attention, a victory bell cuts through the commotion of relief and happiness following a win and concentrates that happiness into a single, passing moment. And then you can start all over again. (Unfortunately, this is where transcendental meditation and dogs finally diverge, as a ringing doorbell might be the only thing that will surely distract a dog from his sun-seeking goal orientation. That and squirrels.)

I like ringing bells. I like thinking about the next bell.

I said earlier that 99 percent of my life has been very, very different from those Chi Psi days at Pat O'Brien's. That means there's a missing 1 percent I need to account for. That's stayed the same. That's for the savoring. You should schedule that too—at least in the abstract. You have to set aside some portion of your time for enjoying what you do and why you do it.

In my life, I've had one all-time "1 percent moment." And in a happy twist of fate, it took me back to New Orleans. It was February 3, 2002, and we had just shocked the mighty St. Louis Rams and their Greatest Show on Turf offense. Deep into the next morning, I couldn't have cared less about schemes, drafts, practices, or training camps. Soon there would be contract negotiations and all the hangovers associated with winning the biggest game in the world.

Until they name Nantucket as a Super Bowl site, New Orleans will be the hangovers home for me. Home of my 1 percent, and the only place in the world where the "next" I needed to focus on was my next Hurricane in Pat O'Brien's.

LOOKING FORWARD
WILL HELP YOU SEE

WHAT MATTERS
IN THE PRESENT.

TEN

MISTAKES

They say that couples start to resemble each other after decades of marriage. I've spent as much time with some of my assistant coaches and staff as any old married couple, and I can happily report that none of them have begun to look like me. (I'm sure they are also happy about this.) But I can say that when you are around the same colleagues day after day, year after year, win after win (and loss after loss), you do start sounding the same. You start speaking the same dialect.

Football coaches, like any other workforce, conform around a certain way of saying things, probably to save time and possibly because we don't have anything better to say. Sometimes it really "is what it is." Believe me, we know we can sound like robots. (As I'll discuss at length in my chapter on communication, that's mostly because none of us wants to give too much away or reveal something to the media that we would prefer to work on in private with our teams—for every "let's circle back" or "looping you in" that you might see over and over again in your emails, we can match you: at the end of the day, it's all about execution, okay? Or it's all about fundamentals. Or it's all about winning. Let's circle back to that later.)

It goes deeper than that, though. I've noticed with some of my long-term colleagues that we'll end up speaking with the same tempo, timing, and inflection. It's a little weird sometimes, but it's also just human nature. We're hardwired for mimicry. If you've had little kids, you might remember how certain words and phrases suddenly come home from the playground. You send your angelic and respectful little kindergartner off to school and they come home one day and call you a butthead. In football, we're together all day, every day. Ten to twelve hours a day is normal for players, coaches, and staff; twelve to sixteen hours a day is typical among the coaches. It is what it is.

The other reason these idioms and sayings take root and stick around is because football is a game of jargon: technical terms, play calls, code words, variations on variations, alerts, contingency plays, and so on. Because the game is played on a clock, we have to smash a lot of information into as few syllables as possible. Efficiency is the mother of these inventions. Sometimes you need a way to cut through and signal that what you're about to say is really important.

All of this is the context for one of my favorite little pieces of football dialect, which has been in heavy usage in any high-functioning team I've been around. It should be a part of your lexicon too (depending on your HR policies). Four words essential to an accountable, healthy, improving operation that is all about sustained success. Four words I made sure I said more than any of my assistants or players.

"I f***ed that up."

Four words that will delight your colleagues (especially any who report to you) until they realize that the expectation embedded in the ownership of error is that they reciprocate when it's their turn.

You gotta say it loud enough for everyone to hear, at least for everyone who was affected by your mistake. It's especially important for people to hear it from their boss. As head coach, it stands to reason that I should say it the most, and loudest. I have the most responsibility and should be the most accountable for high performance. My mistakes affect the most people. But everyone else has important responsibilities too. "I f***ed that up" can become a normal part of our daily conversations—as normal as "Today we're working on the red zone"—and we can be better for it.

It's about honesty and accountability, yes, but it also sets a standard that mistakes can and should be ventilated instead of hidden or lied about. If you have any kind of influence or leadership in your workplace, your blunt admission of error will make it so other people—at or below your level in the hierarchy—can admit it as well. Saying those four words isn't easy at first, especially when you're a rookie or on the margins of whatever team you're on. But here's the truth: You will mess up. You will drop a pass that should have secured a first down. Everyone will see it, including the quarterback. And he might not go back to you that quarter, or even that half, as a result. He needs execution, after all. But a good way to guarantee that he won't try you again for a game or even more is if you deny what happened.

Most important, taking accountability solves the problem. Problem-solving is especially critical during a game. On every play, a lot of things happen very quickly, and as a coach, you have to identify challenges and fix them before the team goes back on the field. When a player says, "I screwed it up, but it was a good play. Call it again and we will crush it the next time," I *love* that. I love when someone takes responsibility, so we don't need a conference to figure out what happened. His decisive ownership of responsibility means that his teammates aren't left wondering whether they have to make some adjustment, which in turn will only make the situation worse. Same thing with coaching. At times, a play caller will call a play looking for a certain matchup. If they get the matchup—great play. If the matchup *doesn't* materialize—bad play. As a play caller, I have said on many occasions, "That was a bad call, my fault. I won't call it again—don't worry about that play because it will not come up again in this game." I've heard from members of the Navy SEALs about their training, and they stress how accountability and good decision-making are critical to their work, especially in situations where time is of the essence. To make smart decisions at crucial times, you need to identify the problem or situation, get accurate information, and be confidently decisive. Excuses and the blame game are major obstacles and have no place in the process. Simply saying that you blew it doesn't erase the mistake. That's already done. But it makes other people trust that you're already working on fixing it, and not dwelling in self-deception.

There was another advantage in being the first to say that I made a mistake. The media often thirsted for me to say some version of the four words to them, and sometimes I did, and while there's nothing wrong with acknowledging mistakes publicly or in some dramatic way, that's less important than acknowledging them quickly. After all, who is (or should be) the person who first realizes that you made a mistake? You. You know it happened, and you probably know why it happened. So be the first to own it. Don't make your coworker have to nudge you into the spotlight. In any event, you're already there even if you pretend you aren't. So don't.

"I f***ed that up." Four words that will earn you loyalty and trust as a leader, or leeway and second chances if you're still in the trenches. A culture of accountability, built on four words that can cut through any jargon. And once you start, others will follow.

. . .

You might be thinking: *If this is all so simple, why doesn't everyone do it?* Because the easiest thing in the world is to blame other people, that's why. It doesn't get more complicated than that. Why do some teams have a different culture? Why do some coaches blame other coaches, and why do some coaches blame their players for their own mistakes? Because it's easy.

You cannot pass the buck like that. It's your job to *get* a player, a teammate, an employee to do it the right way. If he doesn't, then you didn't do your job. As a leader, your job is to fix problems, not create them. Identify the problem, and if the problem is you, then own it and fix it.

Wherever you are in the hierarchy, accountability is one of the best traits to exhibit. There is nothing a head coach appreciates more than hearing someone be accountable for whatever went wrong (and get assurance that it will not happen again). That doesn't *justify* a mistake or bad decision, but it acknowledges that we all make them. An employee who doesn't take responsibility for anything that goes wrong will never garner the respect to be a good leader. I have worked with some people who have all the answers. These people think they know everything, but the truth is that they are closer to knowing nothing (about certain matters) on which they are voicing opinions.

We all know how to take accountability, and we all know that it's the right thing to do, both ethically and in terms of building a functional organization. But sometimes there is a temptation to delay accountability until we feel certain that admitting a mistake on something won't overwhelm the value or security of our role. This calculation simply doesn't stand up to scrutiny. Yes, a mistake on your first day of work looks a lot more damning than when you make one a year later, but on the other hand, your responsibility early on will be so limited that any mistake you make will be contained.

One year when we were heading into the playoffs, Hall of Fame Coach Jimmy Johnson was in Foxborough to do an interview about the Patriots. I asked him to speak to the team and he was beyond great. He told a story about a special teams meeting from his time with the Dallas Cowboys, where Jimmy and Jerry Jones built a championship organization that won three Super Bowls. The meeting was one week before the playoffs began and one of the players dozed off. Unfortunately for him, Jimmy caught him. The lights went on, and, in front of the rest of the team, Jimmy cut the sleepy player on the spot. Talk about sending a message. You should have seen the reaction from our players. One player asked Jimmy a question: "Coach, what would you have done if that was Troy Aikman?" Jimmy replied that he would have nudged Troy and said, "Troy, pay attention." The room exploded with laughter. Jimmy's point was that we are all treated differently depending on how many pelts you have on the wall. Troy, like Lawrence Taylor or Tom Brady, was not going to be released if he dozed off (we will talk about how to handle star players later).

Your responsibilities should curve upward with your tenure and demonstrated ability. If an intern shows up and breaks the coffee maker or dings the starting middle linebacker's truck in the parking lot, that's a shame, but life goes on. They gain everything by acknowledging it, and gain nothing from denying it. Easy for me to say, right? Not really. If you follow that logic through, you'll realize that what I am talking about is an exponential relationship between status at work and responsibility. I am not insulated by having a lot of influence and power at work; I'm especially *exposed*. Therefore, my decisions have to be that much better. When a leader makes a mistake, the whole organization pays for it.

Let me tell you about one of the more agonizing "I f***ed that up"s I have seen.

We were supposed to go 19–0.*

Even before David Tyree's miracle "helmet catch" fueled the New York Giants' comeback (and our crash landing), the 2008 Super Bowl had been strange. The Giants won the opening coin toss and possessed the ball for nearly the entire first quarter. Our record-setting offense had put up thirty-eight points against the Giants in the regular-season finale but didn't set foot on the field in the Super Bowl until a ten-minute drive ended in a field goal.

We scored a touchdown on our first possession, which extended into the second quarter. The tempo of the game got even more bizarre: after an entire quarter, there had been only two drives. One from each team.

From then on, it became a defensive struggle, with neither team sniffing any points until midway through the third. We had the ball, but failed to make any dent in their defense, and found ourselves in fourth down and thirteen to go from the Giants' thirty-one-yard line.

Sometimes you get to big moments and don't like any of your options. This was the biggest moment of all, and all three of our options seemed undesirable.

Our kicker, Steve Gostkowski, was in his second year. He would turn out to be the best in the league for over a decade, but that season had been relatively uneventful for him. Because our offense with

---

* So it's said now. That idea is a little misleading, as it makes all those victories seem preordained or easy in some way, and there is nothing easy about going undefeated, but it's true: we could have gone 19–0, and in our minds, we were well positioned to do it.

Brady, Moss, and Welker had been so good, and because we were so often—and so quickly—in control of games, we had only a few situations where he needed to kick under pressure, and none had been on natural grass. In light of this, I didn't want to take a chance on missing the field goal and giving up the ball with good field position—other than that first field goal of the game, the Giants had struggled on offense. I didn't want to risk helping them out by giving them a head start down the field. That was option one.

Option two was even uglier. We had the best offense in the league, and the best quarterback in the history of the game . . . and nobody wants to punt from the thirty-one. What's the benefit? Gaining twenty yards or so? Or less if the punt isn't carefully placed? That was option two.

So here was option three: Go for it. Going into the game, I did not think the Giants would play as well on the defensive side as they did. All season our offense had dominated, but not on this day. The decision was an inflection point in the game, and had it happened later on or in the fourth quarter, I'd have been less inclined to go for it on fourth and long, but I still hadn't accepted that the Giants defense was playing at the level they plainly were. I held on to my confidence in our passing game longer than I should have. I should have attempted the forty-eight-yard field goal. Option one was the right option.

In my entire career, I have decided to go for it on fourth and ten yards or more while ahead in the game exactly once. That was the one.

I f***ed that up. Nothing more to it. Very simply, our chance of making a forty-eight-yard field goal was better than converting on fourth and thirteen.

I learned my lesson. I wish I hadn't learned it in the Super Bowl.

If I can admit that, then you can admit that you forgot to remove the watermark from that one PDF before it was sent to a client. You can admit you were the guy who left his coffee mug on the conference room table and it left a mark. You can admit you were the last to use that jammed copy machine. One hundred million people didn't watch *your* mistake—and get to watch it again and again and again on YouTube.

My message in the first part of this chapter about the power of acknowledging when you make a mistake is in no way meant to make it seem like it's okay to make those mistakes. Quick, honest acknowledgment of an error is good only if it leads you to make fewer of them in the future. Work is not about discovering yourself. Football is not therapy. Winning happens despite mistakes, not because of them—and the goal, always, is to win.

So, let's take this one step further and talk about the fundamental thing: how to avoid making mistakes in the first place.

I have two big rules about mistakes that I expect my teams to abide by. The first: avoid the big ones. Nobody gets up in the morning and thinks, *Today I'm going to make a mistake that I'll never get over*, but major missteps don't just happen out of nowhere. They happen when we get distracted. They happen when we are too busy worrying about less important problems or minor aspects of the overall challenge that become irrelevant anyway if we mess up. Big mistakes also happen when you cut corners in or downplay your process. Rigor prevents this—especially when you apply enormous rigor to particularly important decisions.

For example: when I hired an assistant coach, I considered it as important of a process and decision as if I were hiring a C-level executive. This person could, and should, be able to handle the entire enterprise if push came to shove. He or she needed to be tested.

The interviews and scrutiny I put coaches like Josh McDaniels and Brian Daboll through were truly rigorous. Days of learning our system (and being tested on it), drawing up plays on a board, and teaching those plays back to us, all while being watched by me and several other staff, monitoring for any signs of breakdown or fatigue. With Josh and Brian, the more we scrutinized, the more they stepped up. They seemed to relish the rigor. And they are now among the best coaches in football.

Don't get me wrong, we had our share of bad hires too. But, looking back, those happened when, for one reason or another, we had to drop the process and rely on hope or a single recommendation—situations where we had to move quickly (or thought we had to) and ended up moving backward, because by jettisoning our rigor, we let bad hires slip through. Decisions based on hope are not decisions at all. They're fantasy stuff—about as rigorous as blowing out the candles on a birthday cake and making a wish. It won't happen. But even if it does, it won't be because of you.

You won't make big mistakes if you do your job. Small mistakes? Hey. That's part of the game. I can live with small mistakes. I have to, because I make them all the time.

My first rule about mistakes might be about catastrophes, but the second one is about something more insidious, something that can hollow out your organization: avoid the ones that happen for the wrong reason.

In my line of work, "the wrong reason" is almost always ego. Anytime someone makes a decision based on their personal brand or to prove to the naysayers that they can do things their own way and succeed, that person will not succeed for long. Sometimes these people are so flagrantly egotistical they come crashing down quickly and look especially foolish while doing so. But, more often than not, the ego-based decision-making will be subtler. It might even be benign. Perhaps you fall in love with a specific way of doing things because it worked before. In football, we can get in a groove in play calling or get ambushed by a team (like the Giants, for instance) because we relied too much on our prior judgments. It's not necessarily laziness, since you'll still be working hard to prepare, but it's a kind of egotistical blindness to the reality that a situation is never the same twice. And you do not honor your past success by trying to re-create it. You simply inhibit the possibility of sustaining success.

The way to avoid this quiet egotism is by committing proactively to adaptation. Don't wait to discover what the new circumstances of any given challenge are—assume that they will be new and prepare for what they might be. Assume change, and constantly adapt. Otherwise, you will get stuck in your old ways and make mistakes for no good reason at all. As Bob Dylan says, "The times they are a-changin'." He's right about that. (In the same song, he also says, "The slow one now will later be fast," and I'm not so sure about that—at least in football the slow ones will always be the slow ones.) Times change in the NFL every season, every week, every day, and sometimes every hour. Embrace it.

I won't call it a "big mistake" because there's a reasonable explanation for what happened, but it's worth diving into why we neglected to draft Lamar Jackson in 2018.

Here's the context: the way the league is structured, it's very hard to use your top pick on a quarterback when you already have an entrenched starter. You can absolutely do it at other positions, where multiple guys will play in any given game—got a good receiver or pass rusher and you want to draft another? Guys will rotate in and out. The quarterback doesn't rotate. Tom Brady doesn't rotate.

We loved Lamar. He was an elite competitor, dynamic playmaker, and ultimate leader. He was not, however, taken first overall, so there was a very good chance we would see him available on the board. We had two picks, the twenty-third and the thirty-first, in the first round—in other words, two chances to take a franchise quarterback. But it wouldn't be a clean transition for Lamar or the Patriots because we still had Tom Brady and we still had no idea how long Tom could keep going. To complicate matters further, Lamar and Tom could not have been more different quarterbacks in terms of play style. Our system had been built around Tom's skills as a conventional pocket passer and expert-level decision-maker. It was his system, as it should have been, and we just could not figure out how to develop Lamar within it or outside of it. It would be extremely tricky to run two parallel offenses, especially when only one would ever really see action in games.

To be blunt about it: We didn't adapt. We failed to make a commitment to adaptation that would have let us find a way to develop Lamar while still winning with Tom. It was possible. It could have been done. We should have tried. But we had our system, and we loved it.

I made a mistake.

Baltimore did not make a mistake. Still, I wonder sometimes: Would the Ravens have selected Lamar if their depth chart included Tom Brady? I doubt it.

In any event, we won the Super Bowl that year. Thanks to all the mistakes we avoided making over the prior nineteen years.

Speaking of Baltimore, one of my favorite stories about mistakes involves the all-time great Ozzie Newsome. One of the top-five tight ends in the history of the game, a Hall of Fame player, and a Hall of Fame executive. An NFL legend in every respect. We missed each other in Cleveland when he was still playing (he retired just as I arrived at the Browns), but he was one of my first hires in scouting and a key person as I embarked on my career as a head coach. I admire him for many reasons, but one particularly legendary thing about Ozzie is that when he was a rookie he had a disastrous fumble in a game that basically sealed the loss. And then? It never happened again.

I don't mean that he never made a mistake with that level of consequence attached to it. I mean he *never fumbled again* for the rest of his thirteen-year career. He had 662 career receptions after that, and I can promise you his success with ball security wasn't because defenses were suddenly going easy on him. (Those were hard-tackling years.) Of all the things that made Ozzie a winner, his determination to never again give the other team a handout was near the top. I am certain he applied that mentality to his exceptional performance as a builder of multiple Baltimore Ravens championship teams—and in drafting Lamar Jackson.

The 2004 Super Bowl, in which we played the Carolina Panthers, had one of the strangest box scores you'll ever see. First quarter: no scores. After three quarters, in step with a prediction from Willie McGinest: "violent." (Mike Minter, who played safety for the Panthers, said that the game would play out "like two trains colliding.") And then there was a sudden and veritable offensive explosion in the fourth, when Carolina scored nineteen points. We barely hung on to win by scoring eighteen in the same quarter. It was a bruising and bloody game; Rodney Harrison had broken his arm and stayed in the game long enough to make the tackle on the next play. It wasn't a coincidence that Carolina finally started scoring only after Rodney had to finally leave the game. It was a strange game.

But not inexplicable.

I had made a mistake going into the game that I would never make now.

The truth is, I have made hundreds of mistakes that almost nobody is ever aware of. Usually this is because they are relatively small, or technical, but they still count, and they can add up. Leaving Dan Klecko, a perfectly good rookie defensive tackle, off our Super Bowl roster that year against Carolina was one of those mistakes. We won, so the mistake is forgotten, but if we had lost I'm sure it would have been discussed. Before the Super Bowl (as before every other game) the head coach has to make a decision on who will be deactivated for the game. By league rules, not every player can be in uniform for a game, so ninety minutes prior to kickoff, each team has to submit their list of ineligible players. That year, the number of players was seven. Sometimes the decision is easy (such as when a player is injured), but other times it is much more difficult and comes down to a judgment call on which player is likely to make the biggest positive impact, or any impact at all, as a backup player: lineman, receiver, or linebacker. I made the decision to deactivate Klecko, a backup defensive lineman who had played in thirteen regular-season games for us, as well as our first playoff game.

Most observers at the time (and most people reading this) were probably wondering: What's the big deal? One backup versus another? Can that really make that big a difference in a Super Bowl? It certainly can, and I should have known better, particularly because of our experience two years earlier, in our first Super Bowl against the Rams, when I saw firsthand how important it was to have extra defensive linemen in a game that would feature plenty of passing (and plenty of pass rushes). The Super Bowl is especially draining because of how hyped up everyone is and because of how long the whole game drags on. The temperature in a packed indoor stadium, such as the Houston stadium that year, also contributes to the fatigue. It wasn't random chance that the fourth quarter of that game turned into a shoot-out. We just couldn't sustain the same level of defensive intensity up-front in those circumstances. We absolutely could have benefited from a young, energetic lineman to spread the snaps out. I made a mistake by not activating Dan Klecko, and we barely survived it.

A mental mistake, such as leaving Klecko off the roster, is different from a strategic error or a wrongheaded plan based on assumptions you shouldn't have made. These strategic errors are errors of judgment, usually made in good faith and with good reason, but with problematic execution. It's important to remember, when such mistakes keep you up at night, that if there hadn't been good reasons, you wouldn't have built a whole strategy around these judgments. Maybe you had bad information, or maybe you made one too many assumptions you shouldn't have—but you didn't just fake your way into a decision. The approach, even if it was flawed, came out of hard work and preparation.

In reality, it is often difficult to know in the moment which kind of error you are making. I'm sure if you had asked me right before that Super Bowl against Carolina why I didn't roster Klecko, I could have given you a coherent-enough explanation.

In retrospect, I wish I had asked myself this question: Is leaving him off the roster something that will specifically help us win the game? Or is it just something I think I can do and still win? It might sound semantic, but one of those answers prioritizes winning, and one of them prioritizes doing things "my way."

Ultimately, we won that game. But we won our first three Patriots championships by a total of nine points. If I had made three or four more errors on par with the Klecko mistake, that easily could have flipped things the other way. When competition is fierce and the margins are slim, only a few mistakes separate a team like the 2000s Patriots from a team like the 1990s Bills.

ERRORS IN JUDGMENT CAN BE PRODUCTIVE ERRORS IF THEY ARISE FROM HARD WORK AND STRATEGIC PLANNING. MENTAL MISTAKES HAVE NO REDEEMING VALUE.

REGARDLESS, THE ONLY WAY FORWARD AFTER A MISTAKE IS TO EMPHATICALLY OWN

THE MISTAKE TO YOURSELF
AND TO YOUR TEAM, AND
THEN MOVE ON IMMEDIATELY.
THINK ABOUT TEAM,
TEAMMATE, SELF.
ULTIMATELY,
DO WHAT IS BEST
FOR THE TEAM—
YOU CAN HANDLE IT.

ELEVEN

COMMUNICATION

I admit that at times I have been uncooperative with the media. In twenty-nine years of press conferences as a head coach, there have been some moments I'd like to have back. I was not good at ignoring questions from reporters that were phrased in a way that was intended to get a specific reaction. In this, I am not unique—I can pretty much guarantee that you've had a boss whose idea of constructive feedback was to pull you aside and ask you something like "Did you think it was a good idea to . . ." or "I'm confused by your decision to . . ." Some passive-aggressive stuff that they think is a slick way to get their point across without seeming like the bad guy. I've been a little curt with an unsuspecting reporter just trying to do his job. There have been times when I've been asked a question and I've just ignored it altogether. (To be clear, that's better than the alternative, which would have led to my being fined.) The media gets annoyed by being stonewalled, but plenty of people—normal people, fans, businesspeople, other coaches, players—over the years have reached out and told me how much they appreciated how I handled some of these situations. Dealing with the media as I have, and for as long as I have, has taught me a good lesson in one fundamental aspect of communication: some people do not talk straight. They think they are cute, but they have an agenda. However you respond to their provocation—and it is a provocation—they'll write the story they wanted to write.

Now, you may be thinking: *How is this relevant?* If you're not a football coach, Adam Schefter isn't calling you. Your flights aren't being tracked by fans wondering if you're taking a job interview somewhere else. Your private life will never be splashed across the tabloid pages. The majority of people will have their name in the newspaper maybe twice: in the local high school sports roundup and in the obituaries. In between, you pretty much hope to stay out of the spotlight, and if you do, most of the time it means you're doing something right.

My job revolves around communication, and the media is a conduit to everyone in the world. Whenever I speak publicly, I am speaking to our players, coaches, organization, and fans, as well as our direct competitors and their fans, coaches, and players.

Talking to the media is different from speaking to the team. However, there are some common threads, and delivering your message effectively is the goal. If I'm talking in front of cameras and microphones, or if I'm talking in front of a mixed group of starters, backups, coaches, assistant coaches, and staff, I need to be able to express my thoughts in a way that makes my message land with a diverse group of people, all of whom have their own experiences, expectations, and ambitions. I do not have enough time in the day to tailor my message to a hundred different people. So I don't. You don't have to either. You'll save a lot of time and prevent a lot of confusion—no one can twist your words if they're consistent.

TOM BRADY

Page 199 is perfect for Tom, who was the 199th pick in the 2000 draft.

Brady was not always a great quarterback—he became a great quarterback because his level of commitment, discipline, preparation, and performance under pressure were outstanding.

On the field, Tom was the absolute best at avoiding bad plays that hurt the offense. During his two decades, we led the league in the fewest offensive penalties, pre-snap penalties, negative runs, interceptions, and sacks.

In the category of "you cannot win until you keep from losing," Tom kept us from losing. And we won a lot of games. Tom's preparation was elite. He went through the game plan five times from Friday morning to kickoff. He always knew what we were going to do and how we would run each play against every defense we anticipated from our opponent. Tom knew the defensive coordinator's tendencies and the tactics used by our opponent in specific end-of-game situations. He recognized favorable matchups quickly. As I told Tom weekly, we would not gain any yards until he got the ball out of his hands. Tom knew how to get the ball (run or pass) to his teammates so they could gain yardage.

Brady was always respectful, but he was the ultimate competitor. After several hundred meetings over two decades with Tom, I can honestly say that his intense desire to win was unparalleled. He never let up in his quest for perfection and success. His greatness and ability made his teammates better.

Tom was hard to coach because he was so well prepared. I loved coaching Brady—he brought out the best in me. He was smart, mentally and physically tough, and the most dependable player I have coached.

Drafting Tom at number 199 was the best decision I ever made.

I have a lot of experience with this. In football, we've been keeping stats about everything for decades (not quite as long as baseball, but our game has changed a lot more than baseball has, so it's not as easy to find the common denominators—good luck running advanced metrics on the 1881 showdown between Harvard and Michigan, especially with a final score of 4–0), but the real explosion in data has been in recent years with the development of next-generation stats. You can go deep into data such as "yards after catch above expectation" or "air yards to the sticks" to get a more granular view of player performance than we've ever had before.

I have a suggestion for a new next-gen stat: TSWMHC. Or, if you aren't in a rush, Time Spent With Media by a Head Coach. I can pretty much promise you I would lap the competition. George Halas didn't have nearly the volume of daily media obligations that we have today. As an NFL head coach, I was required to meet with the entire media group five days a week—on top of appearances and interviews on radio and TV shows, network production meetings, offseason press conferences (especially around the draft), and spring practice. So let's just pause for a moment and do some math: 16 weeks x 5 media sessions per week = 80. That doesn't include six weeks of preseason, the bye week, and postseason (an additional five weeks, if we were successful). Now the number climbs to around 150.

The White House press secretary doesn't have this many meetings and they have a lot more to talk about than any football coach.

By the way, there is one media session I absolutely always wanted to have to attend, but it is a tough one: Monday at 8 a.m. after the Super Bowl. After the most energy-draining game of my life, and staying up all night with the team, family, and friends at the postgame celebration, that 8 a.m. start is a tough one. But one you work all year, and all my life, to attend.

And from all those experiences, good and bad, I have developed a theory about what plays best when you're talking to someone who has a stake in what you say. They want (1) a good, entertaining clip that they can deliver to their consumers, and (2) information nobody else has.

The first one is self-explanatory. The second can be unpacked a bit.

It's not just that new information is valuable per se; it's that when you share something candidly, or exclusively, with someone else, that person will trust you more, because they will feel like you deem them worthy enough to be the special recipient of this info. It feels good to have someone confide something in you. It means they think you, among all the other people who they could have confided in, are the one who deserves to know.

In the history of our league, I'm not sure there is a better example of a coach exhibiting both those rules than Bill Parcells. In 1997, he was between teams, having left the Patriots after taking them to their first Super Bowl in eleven years, and he'd become focused on a long-standing point of contention within the system: that the general manager selected players for the team and the coach built a strategy around what he was given. It was less common back then for anyone to be doing both (you could pretty much assume all coaches wanted more of the former duty, and not a few GMs preferred to perform the latter), but Parcells made his own stance clear one day in a press conference.

"If they want you to cook the dinner, at least they ought to let you shop for some of the groceries."

In other words, the two pieces of the process could not exist independently from one another. A reporter for *The New York Times* who covered the remarks, the legendary George Vecsey, wrote an entire article about the mindset, headlined "Parcells Seeking New

Kitchen": "Many football fans think no coach is worth a first draft choice, but my feeling is that some coaches are always going to be better than most of their peers, and Parcells is clearly one of the best," Vecsey concluded.

Entertaining, clear, and effective.

Parcells's comment was a real risk to say out loud—he was potentially limiting the number of teams that might be interested in his services—but in expressing his expectations clearly, his message was better heard. Any future employer was being told, directly, *This is what kind of leader I can be, and expect to be. Hire me and you hire this perspective. You have been warned.* And by saying it in an entertaining way in front of the media, he guaranteed that everyone would hear it simultaneously. He didn't have to go through back channels.

Entertaining, clear, effective, and *confident*.

The Jets would hire him shortly thereafter, and they let him shop for the groceries. They went to the AFC Championship game after one year.*

No matter what you do every day, you can use communication to your advantage. Think about what you want and how you can get it. Consider how you speak to the power holders, who can make decisions that will benefit you. When you talk to your colleagues, give them good information that will both help them understand things more and build their trust in you at the same time. Be entertaining, clear, effective, and confident in all your communications. And, above all, don't be a jerk.

---

* It should be mentioned that Parcells's comment was also effective because he knew when saying such a thing would have the most impact. He said it right after the Super Bowl, when he could more easily command the headlines of a football media eager to start crafting storylines for the upcoming season.

· · ·

On a team, your voice is one of many. The advice above is all directed toward the way you operate within an organization. It's directed toward the goal of showing how excellent you can be and meshing well with your colleagues. It's directed at standing out and exhibiting confidence.

But there's another side to strategic communications. Knowing when not to speak.

I always get asked after a game: "What did you tell the team?" It doesn't matter whether we win or lose; people want to know, and I understand why. They want to share in a unique moment, a moment of team unity, good or bad. They've seen movies and TV shows, or they've seen *Hard Knocks*, and imagine the remarks of the coach after a game to be either dramatically inspiring or dramatically aggressive. My words might be. But the public will never know, because I'll never tell them. Those are words that I don't want to have to make strategic. I don't want to have to censor myself or tune my words to make them sound right in the ears of journalists who have jobs to do, who aren't paid to win football games but to win attention spans. A cohesive team will always have moments of team-only communication. There will be times when privacy permits some hard truths to emerge. To that point, I will almost never criticize a player or coach in public. That's dangerous business. It might feel good in the moment to direct the spotlight onto someone else and let them take the heat, but there will be consequences. That other man isn't there to give his side of the story, not if you're the leader and you're calling out someone lower on the ladder. Think about what the person on the receiving end of your lecture might think: *Why did he call me out in public instead of in private? Of course I know I made a mistake, and I welcome the correction, but it's just as easy to do it to my face as in public. What's his game here?*

And if you're someone who airs dirty laundry to promote your podcast or salsa brand or whatever: just know it's going to come back, and the other guy will have more time to prepare.

"Right now . . ." is a phrase I recommend you keep in your back pocket for anytime you're dealing with someone like this, someone with an agenda. Use it with your boss who's blaming you for something they did, or with your colleagues who are trying to off-load their responsibilities onto you: "Right now . . . this isn't going to work."

It pulls everything back to reality. Back to the present, and back to the fundamentals.

Even if you do not speak to the media regularly (or at all), some of these tips might be useful in answering questions or talking points that you want to avoid. In my line of work, "Right now . . ." keeps the conversation from veering off into hypotheticals and attempts at headline-making answers. *It's September and you've already lost two games. What does that mean for the season? How many more games can you lose and still make the playoffs? What does this mean for the team as you try to defend your title? Have you guys gotten complacent?*

Right now . . . we're focused on today. Right now . . . we're focused on this week's game plan, this week's practice, this week, period. Right now.

It's simple but effective, like all good strategic communication.

Another simple thing I've picked up is: never repeat words or phrases from the question. If a client asks you why something is late, or if the radio host is asking you why your quarterback is struggling, do not let them set the terms of the communication.

"Why is this late?"

Speak for yourself.

"We've been putting everything we've got into this, and it's coming along great, so I'm confident that when we have it ready for you, it will represent the best efforts of our entire team. And it will be soon."

Of course, I would be remiss if I didn't acknowledge that "speaking for yourself" can sometimes go too far. We once had a running back utter words that I still cannot fathom. He was a rookie, speaking to media for the first time, and a reporter asked him to describe himself as a player.

He put himself—I am cringing as I type this—in the same sentence as Earl Campbell, Jamal Lewis, Bo Jackson, and Fred Taylor.

Really, young man? A Hall of Famer and an All-Pro? Already? I would truly have loved to have my skepticism shoved back in my face, but he ended with fewer career carries than Campbell might have in a single game. I will grant him this: his comment played great with the media. They loved it. And to be honest, it probably boosted his confidence for a while. Or at least induced him to try extra hard to justify his ludicrous statement. But then he actually played some snaps. Unfortunately, his NFL career was short and, in my view, unproductive. My advice is to avoid making these types of predictions, publicly or privately—and let your performance speak for you.

Be entertaining and be new. Don't be insane.

One of my media favorites is Randy Moss. (He's also one of my all-time favorite players, but you already know that.) Randy was a superstar since high school, back before his record-breaking rookie season with the Minnesota Vikings. Every move that Randy made, for years, had been reported on. Some of the coverage had been fair,

THE ART OF WINNING

but some of it had really burned him. Many incidents over many years had given him a level of cynicism that often worked to his advantage. One year, he went several weeks without talking to the media, a direct violation of the league rule that all fifty-three players on a team be available to media in the locker room. Naturally, the media complained to the NFL office, which in turn may have sent a warning down to Randy: be available or be fined. Well, like the rest of us, Randy liked to hold on to his cash. So, there he was in the locker room, amid all the other grown men, more or less clothed, showering, dressing, listening to music, while something like fifty members of the media, wandering around in little teams, went from locker to locker. Camera crews jockeyed for position around the highest-profile players. Everyone was trying to avoid filming background nudity. (It's a bizarre scene.)

"Okay, media!" Randy suddenly yelled out. "You got three questions! Make 'em good!"

Randy cut through the noise and chaos and made his availability . . . available. But it was done on his terms. He was direct and perhaps a tad dismissive. He had simply created an expectation that the media would have to perform as excellently as he just had in order to get what they needed. Randy did his job, so they needed to do theirs. To me, those simple and unmistakable instructions were gold—so much so that I had adopted them myself in press conferences. I was never as eloquent as Randy, but I got my—his—point across. You want to ask questions about the game? Ask good ones. I love football. I want to talk about it, and I will, if I feel that the person on the other end is truly receptive and interested in what I have to say.

That's another core tenet of communication: accountability.

I'm also a fan of Theodore Roosevelt's principle to "speak softly and carry a big stick." Words don't matter much if there isn't something to back them up. Players who do their job well aren't the ones who talk the most about how good they are; they are the ones who are accountable to their goals.

I want to be clear about that: I could have said "who participate in a culture of accountability." (Whatever that means.) But I did not. Teddy didn't say "speak softly and establish a culture of big sticks." He was an individualist. *You* have the voice. *You* need the stick.

It was clear early on in my athletic career that I was not going to have an athletic career. I was never very big as a youth player, and I lacked the natural quickness that had helped my father excel in football. In an industry where excellence is measured on the margins and physical domination is the medium of competition, I would not myself be a "big stick" that could awe these men into submission. But I figured out that there were other ways to inspire fear.

I decided to focus on the first part of Teddy's motto: speak softly. To my mind, this rule has less to do with any specific volume or tenor of your voice and more to do with the implication: when you speak softly, it means other people have to stop talking for you to be heard. It means that other people have to bend their concentration more acutely toward you. You become the focal point, and if you can speak softly in a room full of linebackers, all locked in on your words, then you have created an environment that both solidifies your standing and brings about the ideal circumstances for learning. Yelling has its place. Sometimes you have to force the issue. (Yes, I warned my guys that I could go find better football players down at Foxborough High School once or twice.) But there are rapidly diminishing returns on bluster and empty threats. Exaggeration can quickly tip over into inanity, and if you are constantly hitting one note (and threatening this or that catastrophic punishment) you'll start to lose credibility because you won't be able to follow through on everything you bluster about.

The more genuinely threatening (and therefore more inspiring) way to convey your expectations is *honesty*. Honest communication is authentic communication. When you're a leader—when you have some control over the destiny of your team—then authentic communication fulfills "speaking softly and carrying a big stick." Your job almost certainly resembles mine more than it resembles that of an NFL linebacker. I don't care how many podcasts from fitness guys you listen to, and I don't care about how much you can bench. The most formidable businesspeople I've crossed paths with do not carry themselves like drill sergeants; they wear their authority with more control and command. They speak softly, and the softer they speak, the bigger the stick.

HONESTY IS GOOD.
THERE IS A PLACE FOR
SPEAKING SOFTLY,
AND A PLACE FOR
SPEAKING FORCEFULLY.
EFFECTIVE COMMUNICATION.
DEPENDS ON KNOWING
THE DIFFERENCE.

TWELVE

ADVERSITY

When I think about adversity, I think about a famous poem about football in Ohio. It's about a hardscrabble town and the community that rallies to its football team. It begins, "In the Shreve High football stadium, / I think of Polacks nursing long beers in Tiltonsville . . ." and ends with talk of how, at the beginning of October, the local boys "gallop terribly against each other's bodies" as their fathers watch.

The poem describes a basic orientation toward adversity that, I think, gets to the heart of a certain kind of personality that I have seen in football throughout my lifetime. Some people are inclined, from almost the beginning of their lives, to push forward in spite of setbacks or hard circumstances. I might also describe that inclination as the inclination to win.

My grandparents, like so many others, left impossible hardships in the old country to settle here. They spoke no English, so they relocated where other Croats had settled before, clustered around

THE ART OF WINNING

industrial regions in the Midwest and the Great Lakes. They were working as hard as they could to put food on the table. They had lots of kids, and everyone contributed. They didn't have a choice. My grandfather walked five miles to work every day, and back again at night. My father, Steve, would caddy sometimes as a kid and earned a few pennies in tips—until, that is, he started to play football. Back then football was what the sons of the working people in eastern Ohio did. It was something to do that wasn't merely subsisting, wasn't keeping the lights on at home, something that brought pride to their fathers and mothers, and it was, occasionally, a way to become so excellent at something that they could make their way out of the blast furnaces and slag heaps and go to college. My father was one of those young men. He was good and Bill Edwards recruited him to play football at Western Reserve University in Cleveland, Ohio. My dad could not afford college, but he managed by living in a vacant room in the gym, delivering ice, and doing other assorted jobs to make ends meet. His life was defined by circumstances beyond his control—and he met them head-on. He didn't just meet them; he triumphed over them.

Many, many good football players before and since have come from circumstances just as hard. Some today come from measurably worse. But why did they "make it out" and get to the NFL when others like them, in similar circumstances, never do? What is it about football that seems to help people meet and overcome adversity?

Bill Parcells is the best coach I have ever worked for. His presence and charisma were larger than life, and he had the physical stature to match. He was one of the all-time great motivators and possessed an uncanny ability to squeeze every ounce of potential out of

212

every player and coach on his team. He had every pitch you could imagine and could adapt himself to any player. He could certainly throw some high heat and get in guys' faces when he needed to, but he also had a changeup when it was time for something gentler, and a big, snapping curveball to keep everyone on their toes, including yours truly. He could meet any moment. But even though he had all that in him, his one true obsession was routine. He never deviated if he didn't have to. He was as regimented (and superstitious) as anyone I've ever been around. One of the all-time creatures of habit, he ate at the same Italian restaurant every Friday night during football season—Manny's in Moonachie, New Jersey—and arrived at the stadium at the exact same time every single day. Predictable, familiar segments of preparation. Otherwise known as "consistency."

Consistency lets you tell yourself (or your players) where to be, what to do, and when to do it. Consistency puts you in the best position to weather adversity, by maintaining preparation despite adverse conditions. Over time, this better preparation will yield wins where other people will flounder.

Bill is also passionate about horse racing, both as a fan and as an owner. He's owned many racehorses and named one of them Sunday. It was too perfect. A lot of Bill's identity has been shaped by what happened on Sunday. For all that happens every other day and throughout the year, it all comes down to what happened on the Sunday stage. If the National Thoroughbred Racing Association policy allowed numbers in horses' names, Bill probably would have named that horse Sunday at 1:00, in reference to the standard NFL kickoff time. *Not* Sunday at 4:25 and *certainly not* Monday at 9:00. Bill cherishes consistency almost as much as he cherishes horses.

For coaches like Bill—and those of us who learned from him—consistency of schedule was one of the keys to success, as well as a pleasure in its own right. I cannot imagine what he thinks about our new era of weekly Thursday and Friday games. (As head coach of the Cowboys, he coached in four Thanksgiving games, but that has its own consistency too. Thanksgiving doesn't really creep up on you.) You may have your own opinion on playing football on Thursday nights, but from the perspective of a head coach, it's the definition of adversity.

And what do you do when adversity disrupts your consistency? What happens when the NFL tells you that you have two or three fewer days to prepare for a game? What do you do when your boss calls you at 8 p.m. and tells you that she actually needs the spread-sheet by 9 a.m. the next day instead of next week like she initially said? Complain?

Good luck.

Look past the initial cloud of adversity. There you'll find op-portunities. A lot of people—people who grew up with adversity—know this intuitively. People who come from places where football is something that brings the community together as a way to honor and celebrate hard work. When difficult circumstances arise, look for the advantage instead of dwelling on the disruption. A lot of people know this. But a lot of people don't.

And that's why I like Thursday nights.

For most NFL teams, a typical week goes something like this:

Monday—medical checks, weight lifting, review game film.

Tuesday—day off, injury treatment.

Wednesday—begin preparation for new opponent, receive scouting report, heaviest practice day, practice first and second down game plan—and practice kickoff and kickoff return.

Thursday—watch Wednesday's practice film and make corrections; practice third down, two-minute game plan, punt, and field goal.

Friday—watch Thursday's practice film and make corrections, practice goal line and red area, review the entire game plan, go over special situations, and practice punt return and field goal block.

Saturday—watch Friday's practice film, review day, team walk-through, travel.

Sunday—game day.

Add in all our coaches' meetings and that's the whole game plan, for just around seventeen weeks a year. Deviation is avoided at all costs. Because if there *is* a deviation, everything has to adjust, and we start talking in ways that most people would find puzzling. "This week, Tuesday is a Monday . . . we're going to have two Thursdays . . . we're treating Monday like Wednesday." (What? But yes, that's how we talk, and we understand it. Our families grudgingly play along.)

With Thursday Night Football games, preparation is cut in half. It's rough, but there's no leeway once the game starts. Monday becomes a combination Monday/Tuesday preparation day. Tuesday becomes a combination Wednesday/Thursday, and Wednesday becomes a combination Friday/Saturday. Viewers at home expect to see normal football, despite our process being abnormal. At a certain distance, it looks like more of the same; it looks mostly like football. You'll still see the third downs, the red-zone opportunities, the special situations and GTHI moments. But we have to figure out how to get everyone ready in half as much time. The variation in the NFL schedule never bothered me. We adjusted based on the schedule, but over the course of the season, every team plays the same number of games in the same time frame—with every short week comes a long week and vice versa. Nobody watches a Thursday-night game with sympathy for the players because it's a slightly different schedule. We work hard, but so do you. We don't make the schedule. When it's time to perform, we perform. You pay to watch the games, and we deliver.

When Thursday and Friday games began, most teams lamented the challenge of having to play the NFL's version of a doubleheader. And they aren't wrong—it is worse football. Since all thirty-two teams play the same number of games over eighteen regular-season weeks, everything evens out. With each long week comes a short week and so on. I learned to try to take advantage of every opportunity.

As Ted Marchibroda used to say when I worked for him on the Colts, "Time is only good if you use it."

Aside from the challenge for the players to be ready to play two games in four days, I thought playing on Thursday nights could be an advantage. Most years, we had a good team, and our systems on offense, defense, and special teams were varied. Our opponents never knew what they were going to get from the Patriots. We changed our game plans so frequently, it was difficult for opponents to predict, let alone figure out, what we were going to do in any given week. Coaches told me that we were a tougher team to prepare for than anyone else, regardless of how much time they had. So however much a short week was rough for us, if we did a good job, we could make it harder on our opponents than it was on us.

Other than one team having to spend time traveling, the schedule was the same for both teams. My team didn't make excuses and complain; we just figured it out and tried to be better than our opponent. And there was also the silver lining of playing on Thursday, which was that our team would get a few more days on the other side to prepare for the next game, a few more days than our opponent would have.

Do you notice that I'm not talking about making things better for yourself? I'm not talking about what's good for you or best for you or anything like that. I'm talking about accepting adversity on its own terms, especially when it's something that other people in the same situation are also experiencing.

The guys I've been around who grew up in tough circumstances know about this kind of acceptance, because it's what they had to do. Back on the high school football fields, they didn't dwell on whatever chaos or injustice was endemic to where they grew up—they just focused on the fact that, if they could get past it, show up, practice, and perform, then that itself would separate them from the other kids who couldn't. Competition isn't kindness. Adversity is not a test of morals; it's a test of mettle.

Coaching is a profession and a career. Football is a game, but the competition is serious, and severe. If you visited an NFL training room the day after a game, you could very well see a scene that resembles a hospital triage ward. And while the stakes aren't close to what our armed services shoulder, there are similarities in process and structure. There are also similar demands on your capacity to subordinate yourself to the overall team. The best units, and teams, are regimented, structured, and disciplined. Once the weakest are weeded out, that environment breeds intense camaraderie I haven't seen anyplace else. Players who stand in the huddle with one another prepare to engage in hand-to-hand combat in a violent game. Training staff ready themselves to provide care. Coaches sacrifice family time, working late into the night trying to come up with the best red-zone plays. It's a different life. The harder it is, the closer we grow. If we didn't, our team would fall apart in a moment.

Bill Parcells and Vince Lombardi both coached at West Point. Paul Brown, who refined the football playbook, segmented practices, specialized assistant coaches, and innovated many other aspects of the game we take for granted now, was a lieutenant in the US Navy. Tom Landry was a lieutenant in the US Army Air Corps. George Halas served in World War I *and* World War II. Andy Reid's father and uncle were both in the navy during World War II. His father, Walter, was a first responder at Pearl Harbor.

This is just a sampling of some of the major figures of the NFL, and there's no doubt in my mind that their exposure to military culture influenced not only their coaching styles but football in general. How could it not? Once you see it up close, it's impossible to forget.

I was born into a military way of life too, established and reinforced by my father, Steve, who served in the United States Navy in both Europe and the Pacific. I was aware of this part of his history, and later on, as I grew up around the Naval Academy football program in which he coached, I came into contact with many more great leaders who brought the lessons of the service into the sport.

One clear indication of that influence is in a coach's obsession with scheduling every minute of every day. We like to wring the maximum potential out of everything we can control, and that includes time. But as in the military, as committed as we are to our processes, flexibility is a nonnegotiable necessity. "Adapt or die" isn't literal in football, but "adapt or lose" is. I love President Eisenhower's famous quote about planning: "Plans are useless, but planning is indispensable." In other words: If you have a plan, you might lose. But if you don't have a plan, you will *definitely* lose. Pick your path.

In 2010, our week sixteen game at Buffalo fell on December 26, so we all got to have our Christmas mornings at our homes before leaving the wrapping paper and eggnog behind and flying to Buffalo to spend the night together as a football team. It's one of many realities of working in the NFL that strains families and is hard to sell to your team, especially when so many of your players are just starting families and have young kids at home, but the strain is made a little easier when we win.

Thankfully, we did. With a completed 1 p.m. game in Buffalo and a short flight, we were set to be back in Foxborough by nine—early enough to finish up some Christmas festivities. There was only one problem. A snowstorm in Boston prevented us from flying back. Then one problem became two. Not only could we not fly back to Boston, but a major youth hockey tournament was taking place in Buffalo at the same time, so hotel rooms were impossible to find. Not even the Belichick Travel Agency could save the day; when I took stock of the situation, I realized we had a few buses at our disposal . . . but nowhere to go. It didn't help matters that the old Ralph Wilson Stadium was a run-down relic from another era and not the kind of place where it was comfortable to loiter on a cold winter night. Bear in mind that we were a group that lived every day according to a script. Everything we did was purposeful and planned. Nowhere on that script was scrambling for hotel rooms in Western New York because of a blizzard. The day after Christmas.

It was a disaster.

How would you feel in my position? Frustrated? Helpless? Desperate to find someone to blame? Maybe you're already thinking about something similar that's happened to you at work. I wouldn't be surprised—in most organizations, this kind of thing is to be expected. Everything goes bad, all at once. One unit of adversity (snowstorm) gets amplified by the shoddy and unprepared reactions of the decision-makers, and suddenly a cascade of failures starts to flow all over the organization, starting at the top.

What would you do? Would you vent to someone? Would that make you feel better?

What I did, what made me feel better, was looking around and seeing that we had built an organization full of people who could be held responsible for finding solutions. The cascade cannot begin if it doesn't start from the top. We had a plan; the plan was now junk. We had to adapt.

So we bused eighty miles to downtown Rochester and found a hotel there. No matter that the lobby was under construction—the rooms were clean and comfortable, and we were set for the night.

That would have been a perfectly suitable conclusion to the challenge we had faced, a challenge that was totally out of our control. But that's not when the night ended. Because our team was a real team, full of people who had risen above any number of tough circumstances and always came closer together as a way of pushing forward, we turned the Rochester field trip into one of the best nights we'd ever had.

A block from the hotel was a restaurant called Dinosaur Bar-B-Que, the quintessential place for a bunch of football players to visit after a game. We took over the restaurant and spent hours eating, drinking, and bonding. A total throwback night. You'd have thought this was our plan all along—a team outing, with as many ribs and beers as we could consume. (If players were ever going to drink on company time, worry-free, the coaches figured, then this would be it. We might even join in.) If we had to be away from family for not one but two nights on Christmas weekend, this was the ultimate consolation.

What does this all mean for you? That there's a good spot waiting for you in Rochester for barbecue and beers? Not really (although it's true). The lesson is that when inconveniences inevitably hit, you still have options. I would like to tell you that you can choose the attitude that you'll take, once the snowstorm messes everything up, but the deeper truth is that you have already selected your attitude, now and every day you go to work. You select your attitude toward adversity before adversity ever comes. You choose to prepare, to be consistent, and to be team-oriented when those choices are boring. Not when they're exciting. It's too late for team bonding if you choose that path only when the snowstorm hits. Choose it every day. Adopt the posture of people who have grown up with adversity, either thrust upon them or invited into their lives through self-sacrifice and discipline. If you do, you will be ready. The plan might not work, but a man with a plan will find a way to make something work. He already has a head start.

And along the way you might just get to witness Tom Brady out–beer chug the entire team in Rochester. There are worse ways to spend the day after Christmas.

ADVERSITY IS UNIVERSAL. GET OVER YOURS BEFORE THE OTHER PERSON GETS OVER THEIRS.

LOOK BELOW THE SURFACE OF ANY CHALLENGE AND YOU WILL FIND ADVANTAGES.

THIRTEEN

CONFIDENCE

learned a new word while writing this book that I will probably forget after I've finished. It has too many syllables to be useful outside of a laboratory or a hospital, but there's just no other word precise enough to describe what we're going to talk about.

Without further ado: "epiphenomenon." It refers to something that happens at the same time as, or as a result of (the "epi"), some other thing happening (the "phenomenon"). I'll give you a football example: if we establish the run, our play-action game will work better. Those two things happen in concert, but one depends on the other, and the relationship doesn't go both ways.

Confidence is an epiphenomenon. It doesn't exist in a vacuum or independently of everything else. It's relational. And yet these days confidence has become a product people think they can pick up off a shelf. I've heard it all over the years: confidence at work, confidence in dating, confidence in everything. Come on down and pick up your confidence, no strings attached.

Here's the truth: You cannot buy confidence. You cannot learn it, you cannot teach it, and you sure as hell won't get it from reading this chapter or this book. As far as I'm concerned, confidence isn't even something to strive for; it's something that you exhibit when you strive for something in the right way.

But that's not very selling, so my publisher would probably prefer me to put it this way: I can't force you to be confident, but I can help you understand where it comes from.

Bill Parcells rivals Yogi Berra for quotable quotes, and one of my favorites is germane to this very issue: "Confidence is born of demonstrated ability."

I'll leave the grammar lesson behind soon (along with the vocabulary lesson), but I think it's important here to point out that in that quote, Coach Parcells subordinates "confidence" to "ability"—*demonstrated* ability, actually. Confidence does not precede action. It does not come before doing. It comes *from* doing. Not saying, believing, or hoping. Doing. Not hoping the other guy messes up or falls down. Demonstrated doing. Or in the parlance of football (and any other physical activity or mental activity, or any activity at all): practice.

Practice does not make perfect. (Nothing does.) But practice makes confidence. You practice the same skill 500 times a day. You practice doing it different ways. You practice the back shoulder pass, and then you practice it 499 more times. You rehearse for a recital. You repeat your opening lines in the elevator before you step out into the office. You do mock presentations. You run different models, you tweak the models, you tweak your tweaks, and then you run the models all over again. And in the process, confidence emerges, epiphenomenally. (Okay, that was the last time.) It is real and it is powerful. A football player is not going to genuinely believe he can compete in the NFL until he does it in practice, and then in live game action. Nor will his teammates or coaches believe that he can. He can fake it—oh, can he ever fake it—but no one will buy it. You may perform well in a familiar setting, but what happens when the contingencies add up? If your confidence emerges under only the most special of circumstances, it wasn't confidence to begin with. Confidence is something that other people can see, and trust, even during everyday stuff, because it's something that is secondary to what you are actually doing in any moment. So, before you tackle the hard stuff, you better know the easy stuff. How to deal with the person who sits next to you. How to deal with your boss. How to deal with selfish people. How to deal with stupid people. How to deal with the unexpected. The contingencies are all out there. If they aren't with you daily, they will be at some point. How confident you are in your ability to navigate them will play a part in your success.

If I had to pick one sentence that summarizes my coaching philosophy and how I evaluated myself in my job it would be this: "Practice execution becomes game reality." My players have heard me say that hundreds of times—because it is the absolute truth. When a player can execute a skill on the practice field against another competitive player with consistent success, he is capable of implementing that skill in a game. Conversely, if a player cannot consistently execute in practice, the chances of having a successful play in the game are close to zero. Each individual player builds his football fundamentals through practice repetition. If done properly, the player will be successful at his position. If those fundamentals are not completed properly, or repeatedly, they won't become good habits. They will in fact become *bad* habits! It's why any golf pro will caution you about going to the range just to hit balls. What you practice at the range becomes what you do on the course, and if you're just trying to hit as hard as you can, you'll take that strategy to the actual game, with poor results.

Remember what I said about football intelligence, or FBI? Football intelligence is directly related to confidence and demonstrated ability in a way that IQ isn't. It's a bit like the difference between being savvy and being sophisticated. Nothing wrong with the latter, but it doesn't have anything to do with winning.

You may not associate football playing with a form of genius. I do. Sorting out the mayhem that occurs on a football field is kind of like solving one big math problem. Solving it with abnormally large, athletic, aggressive men directing their bad intentions toward you is like one big *advanced* math problem. (Also, no one can hear anything because a crowd of many thousands of people is screaming with such intensity they'll lose their voices the next morning. Also, it's somehow snowing and raining at the same time.) Very few people can compete in these conditions. Even fewer people can compete, solve the problem, and win.

I put a massive premium on football intellect, right up there with toughness and basic positional skill. If you play defense but go out of your way to avoid contact, you can't play for me. If you're a wide receiver and can't get open and catch the ball, you won't make the team. Simple, right? Football intelligence counts just as much.

Don't get me wrong. I'm not against generalized intelligence. It helps with anything you do, football or otherwise, and if you don't have it, you can get yourself into trouble (I've seen promising careers of young people collapse because their general life skills were so badly lacking). But in my line of work, high IQ itself doesn't necessarily correlate to a person's ability to contribute to a winning performance where we need it most: the scoreboard. Nor does a high

IQ necessarily generate confidence in teammates and colleagues. When Bill Parcells said what he did about confidence emerging from demonstrated ability, he wasn't saying that's how it ought to be. He was saying that's how it is.

Belief in yourself is just the beginning. Of course, nothing happens without that. But to ascend to where you really want to be, you have to care more about the trust that your peers have in you. And you in them. The structure that best exhibits confidence is a bridge: each component depends on every other component, and they all trust one another, resulting in something much greater than the sum of its parts. Every truss and beam and cable doing its job in engineered harmony. Just like the one north of the end zone at Gillette Stadium.

WHAT CONFIDENCE ISN'T

Confidence and humility aren't mutually exclusive. You can be sure of yourself and not be a know-it-all. You can know you're good and still know you can be better. (In fact, you must.)* People who tell you how great they are, who act like they have it all figured out, are not confident. Leave it to others to diagnose your confidence level; real confidence is something they can see better than you can.

So how do we know real confidence? How can we separate out the fake stuff from the real?

Here's a rule of thumb: follow responsibility, in others or in yourself. Responsibilities tend to gather around confidence. Are you

---

* Similarly, real confidence doesn't have to go up and down with wins and losses. Losing doesn't have to mean losing your confidence. It means accepting that you don't have all the answers. We see things for what they are. We've got a good team. But we weren't one yesterday. We just didn't play well.

doing the exact same job, with the exact same expectations, that you did when you started? Or have you asked for more?

Darrelle Revis was one of the most confident players I've ever coached. He was the prototypical cornerback who had it all: every physical and athletic measurable that teams covet, plus elite FBI. He was bound for the Hall of Fame well before we got him on the Patriots in 2014. His speed and agility weren't what they used to be—by then he was in the latter chapter of his career—but still Revis played with supreme confidence. His instincts couldn't be copied or even learned.

Something that most fans fail to appreciate is that the two sides of the ball call upon fundamentally different characteristics, and that reality has deep implications for personnel: offensive football is assignment-based and defensive football is reaction-based. The offense has a play and has the ball. They start the play, and the defense works off that.

Revis was the rare defensive player who scrambled that binary. He reacted so quickly and instinctively that he often erased, and altogether reversed, the reaction aspect of playing defense. While most players were trying to figure out where to go, he was already there, playing as if he knew more about what the receivers were doing than they did. Offenses had to react to *him*—and, most of the time, avoid him at all costs.

If I had to isolate one skill that is most closely related to generating confidence it would be foresight. Some people, like Revis, have astonishing powers of perception and awareness, and they work to exploit those powers. The rest of us, meanwhile, gain foresight by practicing, preparing, and studying. You have to know what's coming. A lot of times, a hockey goalie can't even see the puck coming at him because his vision is blocked by multiple bodies standing between him and the shooter. He has to rapidly read the situation in front of him but also be prepared in advance to know what paths the puck *might likely take.*

How quickly do you track your pucks? Can you track them when there are obstacles, or only when you have clear vision? Can you guess in advance what the likeliest paths might be, even before the game begins?

When you accept that responsibility, when you know you have prepared for the problem and put yourself in a position to practice the solution, you know that the seed of confidence has been planted.

CREATING CONFIDENCE

Our 2002 season opener against the Pittsburgh Steelers was the first game ever played at Gillette Stadium. The last time we had faced each other was in the AFC Championship game the previous season, when we took the win, 24–17. That was a massive upset, a matchup the Steelers would probably have won seven times out of ten, if not more. For the past fifty years, the Steelers had consistently been in the upper echelon of NFL teams. They had a formula, were very confident in it, and stuck with it (they still do), as well they should. Especially defensively. They were loaded in 2001 and again in 2002, and we couldn't run the ball in the championship game. We tried (eleven carries in the first half for barely two and a half yards an attempt), and we didn't like our chances of running the ball in '02 any better.

But one thing was different between our opening-day game and the previous season's AFC Championship game. Now we were champions. We had confidence.

The useful thing about confidence is that it's kind of like a currency: you can spend it. Yes, you need to be judicious. And yes, if the results are bad, you will be accused of overconfidence. But that's part of the game. That day against the Steelers we decided to spend a little of the confidence that we had won against the Greatest Show on Turf several months earlier. We did something we had never done and what few teams ever do until time in the game is running out: we went no huddle and called twenty-five consecutive pass plays. We decided to throw the ball until they showed they could stop it, which they couldn't, and because of that our confidence grew with each play. At a certain point, the Steelers knew what we were going to do (pass the ball), we did it, and we got better for it. We won the game, our first in Gillette, 30–14.

The rest of the season ultimately didn't pan out like we wanted it to, but we began building a fundamental team confidence through games like that one against the Steelers. That confidence would carry us through two more decades of winning.

Almost the exact same thing happened four years later, with a few of the same key offensive players from the Steelers game, on a Monday night in Minnesota. The Vikings had the best run defense in the league; no team had scored more than seventeen points on them yet that season. Rather than beat our heads against the wall doing something just to adhere to an old football adage—"gotta establish the run"—we were realistic with ourselves. Our confidence didn't rely on any outsized sense of our capabilities. Instead, it was born out of our demonstrated ability in practice and in other preparation, which in turn permitted us to know and accept our relative strengths and weaknesses. Instead of creating a game plan out of caution and avoidance, we decided to rely on confidence as we had so many times before. We skewed almost as far in the pass-only direction as we did in that Steelers game. The Vikings defense had great confidence, but it was only in playing one way: stop the run in early downs and get after the quarterback in obvious third-down passing situations.

We abandoned the run before the game even started.

We threw the ball on forty-three of the fifty-eight plays in the game and won, 31–13. They did indeed do a good job of stopping our run game.

Make sure you develop confidence in more than one thing. Have a plan B and a plan C. As good as the Steelers and Vikings were on defense, plan A wasn't enough. Having just one plan prepared would have left our overall confidence shattered when it wasn't working out. There's no reason to take that risk.

TOO MUCH OF A GOOD THING

We've covered confidence (and the lack thereof), but a chapter on this subject isn't complete without hitting on confidence's sneaky evil cousin: overconfidence. As much as I value confidence in my players, and seek to generate it throughout the organization, I hate overconfidence. That can be a tough line to toe. And I've had to.

By the late 2000s, that photo wall I told you about a few chapters ago was beginning to get crowded. We had fielded a lot of great teams with a lot of great players who had made a lot of great plays. We had to start stacking photos. But we weren't stacking championships. We did for a while—three in four seasons between 2001 and 2005—but success is all relative, and each season begins anew. By 2010 we were six seasons removed from a title. It was officially a drought. No matter that we had been a playoff team multiple times, lost in an AFC Championship game, and went 18–0 but lost in a Super Bowl. For most teams, those six years would have been the glory days, rings or no rings. For us, they were good, but not good enough. I had to act.

Entering the 2010 season, we had only three players left from our 2004 Super Bowl–winning team: Tom Brady, offensive tackle Matt Light, and running back Kevin Faulk. Only seventeen players remained from the 2007 team that had set records but lost the Super Bowl. Everyone else had joined within the past two years. Winning so much between 2005 and 2009 had given players confidence that we *could* win games, but none of them had achieved our ultimate goal of winning it all—a textbook case of overconfidence. It was as if they thought they'd scaled the mountain like all those guys in the photos. Their sense of themselves and of their team was inflated. It was one thing to have people resting on their laurels, but in this case the laurels weren't even their own.

So I gave them a kind of facelift.

I took down all the photos. It was drastic and, frankly, tough to do. Those photos told a story of greatness, of what we aspired to. For years, everyone was used to seeing what amounted to a wallpaper of Patriots football legends. Going from that to bare white-painted walls was a shock to the system. Especially to those of us who had been there for the first run of Super Bowls.

But the message had to be, and was, clear: you can't be grandfathered into a championship mentality or reputation.

That's no insult or slight to anyone. Many of you joined, or aspire to join, a company or organization based on its track record of success. You are attracted to success and wish to prove yourself in a competitive environment. You should want to join a winner because that's where your best wins will come out. That means learning about the organization, its past winners, and the expectations and specific culture.

But just because you're part of the future, don't let yourself start thinking you were a part of the past. You can't live off others' accomplishments. Even though the people who hired you want to believe they hired the next generation of excellence, and even though out-siders might associate you with whatever breakthroughs, awards, or brand awareness that preceded you, those accolades are not yours. Neither is the confidence. I don't care if you won the starting QB job or landed the plum open position at Nvidia. Those other people in the program demonstrated it. You haven't. Perhaps that makes you mad. Okay, then. Demonstrate ability, and confidence—and success—will follow.

When we won our first title in 2002, Julian Edelman was fifteen years old. In 2010, going into his second season, Julian said this about the blank walls where the famous photos used to hang: "I wasn't on those teams, so I can't even say I was a part of anything like that. We're in training camp trying to build our own team and our own identity." One of Julian's many great qualities was his self-awareness. He was not one of those guys living in someone else's glory. I do not think it's a coincidence that over the next decade, Julian went about ensuring that all those missing photos repre-sented only half of our eventual six championships. And along the way hundreds of new photos (dozens of himself) filled those walls again. Do you think that gave Julian confidence to win again and again? To be a Super Bowl MVP?

You know my answer.

One coach who I admired—"revered" might be a better word—was Bob Knight. I learned a lot from Coach Knight, and the most important point he made that helped me do my job was simply this: If your team is overconfident, or takes the opponent lightly, that is the coach's fault.

I firmly believe that! In my career with the Giants and Patriots, out team was favored in most games and in almost every game in our playoff years. My job was to make sure the team felt that the game was an even match or that we had to play our best game to win. I hammered this message to the team and to the media. I did my best to make every team appear to be a major challenge to defeat. At times, it was an acting job. In my heart, I often didn't really think that our opponent could defeat us, but I *did* think that we were capable of playing poorly and losing. If that happened, and it did occasionally, I knew it was my fault. Period! When we underachieved and lost to a "lesser team," I knew that I had not done my job that week.

The job of a leader is to get his team in a confident mental state, but not overconfident. Finding that perfect edge is sometimes tricky, but that is ultimately the goal. As a spectator, when I watch a game and observe that a team is really ready to go, I know that the coach and coaching staff have done a good job and found the right edge.

CONFIDENCE PERSONIFIED

You know that I can't leave it there. There's someone else who really helped rewrite the script on confidence in a way that might never be matched.

Here's a Tom Brady story I've never told before. It was Tuesday night, September 25, two days after our starting QB Drew Bledsoe was severely injured, and Tom was being elevated to start for us. He was in the office late, watching film, meeting with coaches, and preparing for his first opportunity to lead our 0–2 team. It had to have been around 9 p.m., long after any of the few players who opted to be at the team facility on their day off had departed. As he was leaving the old Foxborough Stadium, he stopped to chat with someone in the hallway, who asked him how he was doing, how it had been the past few days, and what it had been like coming into the previous game in relief of the injured Bledsoe in the fourth quarter of what ended up being an offensively feeble 10–3 defeat.

Tom's reply about coming in started along the lines of "It was okay, it was good to play . . ." Just about what you'd expect to hear from someone in his position. But he didn't leave it there. He went on to say something that has stayed with me—and with the Patriots organization—for years.

"If I'd played the whole game, we would have won by forty."

I didn't take his comment as brash or arrogant, even for a kid who had never started an NFL game. It was a new standard of confidence, cultivated from hours, months, and years of work. His understanding of himself, his teammates, our scheme, our opponents, and the game allowed him to feel fiercely self-assured, and he wasn't afraid to put himself out there to back it up. Plus, he didn't say it in front of the cameras or the fans; he said it late at night in an otherwise abandoned hallway to a colleague, privately.

I loved it.

"We would have won by forty."

Even now it makes me laugh. *Forty*, Tom? Really? Despite the fact that we had scored a grand total of twenty points in our first two games?

The thing that struck me the most, though, was one choice of word.

We would have won by forty.

Not "I'd have thrown for four hundred yards and five TDs . . ."

WE.

His confidence was all about the team, and about results.

What screams Tom Brady more than that?

And wouldn't you know it, five days later, when Tom got that first start, we won, 44–13. Not quite forty. But winning by thirty-one will do a lot for a team's confidence.

CONFIDENCE AND HUMILITY ARE TWO SIDES OF THE SAME COIN, BECAUSE BOTH ARE BASED ON HONEST SELF-ASSESSMENT.

CONFIDENCE IS NOT COMPLACENT. IT IS VISIBLE ONLY IN ACTION, AND IT IS DEVELOPED AS A SIDE EFFECT OF WORK AND PREPARATION.

FOURTEEN

CHANGE

If you close your eyes and try to imagine the most challenging moments at your job, I bet none of them take place on Monday morning. How could they? Nothing has happened yet! You know what to do on Monday morning. You know the routine. You know who's going to be at the coffee machine at 9:15 a.m., who will want to talk about Sunday Night Football (and their fantasy team), and what time to put in your order at Chipotle so that you don't have to wait in line at lunchtime.

In football, we call that being at first and ten. It's the most common situation we have. Everything starts on first and ten. Every drive, every half, every game. No matter how bad your team is, you can't start any worse than needing ten yards.

And guess what: we don't spend nearly as much time as you might think on first and ten. We know first and ten like you know Monday morning. Instead, we spend time on the situations that we don't know, and situations that we don't even know we'll ever see. Because those situations are what make or break games, and seasons. Real wins and losses don't take place on Mondays; they take place at unexpected and off-script moments. Think: third and seventeen. Think: down by nine points with three minutes in the fourth quarter. Think: the Friday-afternoon bad news that your boss sent just before turning off his phone and driving away to his lake house, or the Thursday-morning panic initiated by the Stock Exchange of Hong Kong opening, or the Tuesday lunch with your old colleague who's going through some drama, or the late-night rush to finish a project so that you can get enough sleep to review what you've done the next morning. Those are the situations that make or break your year, your quarter, or your career.

Every play in practice, every play in the game, every down and distance, everything obscure that's come up in other games, are all potential paths to victory. But we couldn't spend any time looking at them if we're just hung up about what's happening at first and ten. Focusing on the predictable and familiar minimizes our creativity and encourages us to develop a simplistic understanding of the game. In reality, every game starts the same, but after that first kickoff, every game develops differently. As a team, we never know for sure where we're going to be when it's our turn to perform. Our strategy changes drastically depending on location, score, and time. So that's what we practice. Reps in certain, but rare, situations are reps that diminish uncertainty overall. We know, going into a game, that we'll be surprised, so we practice those situations.

At some point in practice, in between two scheduled periods, I will randomly call out a situation, and everyone involved immediately runs to their position and we play football.

Say I call out "field goal." The FG team, and their counterpart, the FG block unit, will both go on the field for an FG attempt. The kicker probably hadn't been warming up on the sidelines expecting to kick—exactly how it would happen if, for instance, we returned an interception for a TD in an actual game. The next play would be a kick, and no one would have been necessarily expecting it.

There is no advantage to be found in focusing on the inevitable and the given. Everyone prepares for Monday morning. Everyone prepares for first and ten. Don't bother. Prepare for what's unlikely to happen. Prepare for change.

Sudden swings in action are one of the easiest things to practice because in the most basic sense, it's about staying ready.

Even if you're a star performer and have a secure position, you should be thinking about what it might look like if your organization folded tomorrow. What would you do? Where will you be? Who will you call? What will you say? Who's ready to be their best at that unplanned moment?

The same works in reverse. Perhaps our offense just turned the ball over and now our defense has to stop the bleeding. Or our defense intercepted a pass and now the offense must spring into action. No warm-up, no time to review everything. Do we just run a few nondescript plays and punt it right back, satisfied at least with giving our defense a breather? Or do we extend the momentum, score a TD, and really tilt the game in our favor?

Think about any football game you've watched. Did the key play occur on a second-quarter first-and-ten play from the forty-yard line? I doubt it. Just like your day probably isn't defined by the first thing that happens or whatever your table setter is. That's why the team needs to know about situational football, because this is where most games are won or lost. (Remember, more games are lost than won.) Some teams are great situational teams, and some are poor. I can say with confidence that our handle on situational football was the biggest single factor in our sustained winning with the Patriots.

Understanding every situation you could be in, and there are hundreds of them, is the difference between winning and losing. In golf, tee shots are important. Long and straight is helpful, but there's no correlation between launching drives three hundred yards down the middle of the fairway and making short putts. Or long putts. Or pressure putts to win the tournament. Or successfully getting out of the woods when you do hit that errant drive and saving par. They're completely different skills, and to win you need them all. When elite golfers practice, they don't just stand on the driving range and bang out drive after drive, all day long. Great golfers practice hitting all fourteen clubs in their bag.

It might seem unrealistic to prepare for every possible situation, and that's true. That's why we have to rely on our experience—and the experiences of other teams that we can study—to create a core of decisive situations that might happen. We study other teams and other games and learn from what other teams did well, and poorly—we call them "How Not to Do It" meetings. Players have told me that when they first came to our team and first sat in these meetings, their initial thought was *Why is he talking about what some other team did wrong?* But the more they experienced them, the more I continued to pound away at the importance of situational football, and the more we won because of it, the more they understood. The virtuous circle of winning.

"Remember when we had this exact situation come up three years ago?" I can promise you if you're in a position to say those words at work, you'll be in a position to win. Don't worry about not having a long career to draw from. Look to elite performers and elder statesmen in your field; listen to them when they tell old war stories. Read memoirs, listen to speeches, ask your colleagues. Learn.

•   •   •

You aren't reading this book to learn about clock management best practices or the finer points of keeping a team out of field goal range. So I won't go too deeply into those kinds of specifics. But I have two examples to share, both from Super Bowls, and both plays from a phase of the game I love: special teams.

In the 2010 Super Bowl, the New Orleans Saints and head coach Sean Payton pulled off one of the gutsiest play calls in NFL history—not a razzle-dazzle double reverse or all-out blitz on Peyton Manning, but a surprise onside kick to start the second half. To my knowledge, that had never been attempted before (and hasn't since).

Onside kicks are usually reserved for teams in desperation mode at the end of the game. The kicking team is attempting a comeback, there's very little time left, and it's their only realistic chance to possess the ball enough times to catch up. With recent rule changes, it's almost a stretch to call the kicking team's chances "realistic." In the 2023 season, just over 5 percent of onside kicks were successful. But it's the last arrow in the quiver.

With half of a closely matched game remaining, 99 percent of coaches would kick off conventionally, play conventionally until they were out of options, and then . . . lose conventionally. For Payton to make the unconventional call, in front of 100 million viewers, put him in a direct line of fire. But he did it. And the Saints executed a onetime situation better than the Colts. They recovered the kick, got another possession for their offense, scored one of the only two touchdowns of the game on that drive, and won the Super Bowl. In a game with Peyton Manning, Drew Brees, and numerous other Hall of Famers, the most memorable play went down with all of them standing on the sideline.

No game is decided on one play. But no matter how much we might intellectually understand that there are 150 other plays that could determine any one game, we always remember the biggest ones.

At the Patriots, we had our share of special teams greatest hits, most of them courtesy of Adam Vinatieri and his kicks through freezing temperatures, drifting snow, and expiring game clocks. But this one was the odd special teams highlight that left Adam on the sidelines. Instead, the star of this situation was our hands team. The hands team is composed of our most dependable special teams players and handlers of the football. They practice recovering onside kicks every week despite the fact that it rarely comes up in a game. But when it does happen, the game is most likely on the line. Just ask the Colts.

Late in the 2005 Super Bowl, we had a 24–14 lead on the Philadelphia Eagles. With 1:48 left in the game, when the Eagles scored to close the gap to 24–21, our hands team took the field for the first time all season. That's the most extreme case of situational football I can think of—we had practiced literally all year and got this one opportunity, on a play unlike any other, to do our jobs with a Super Bowl championship at stake.

The Eagles gave it their best attempt at an onside kick, but we recovered. It wasn't quite "game over" because we had a couple more situations to execute. But we had the advantage, no doubt: we held the lead with under two minutes remaining and didn't need to score. We didn't need to make a first down. We just had to work the situation, which meant eating time off the clock and forcing the Eagles to use their time-outs, and run a few disaster-free plays. We elected to run the ball three times and made the Eagles exhaust all three of their time-outs.

The more aggressive approach would have been to attempt a pass on one of those snaps, in order to pick up a first down, and then the Eagles wouldn't have had the ability to stop the clock. We would have been kneeling on the ball and the game would have been over. Teams do that all the time, but in that situation, I didn't think it was the right approach. Too risky. When things get to that point, time is more important than anything, even possessions. Everything came down to one final special teams play. Perhaps the least glamorous play in all of football.

Remember earlier when I was describing how pro golfers use the range versus how most other people do? Well, I see a direct correlation to punters. Not every punt is of the "kick it as far and straight as you can" variety. In fact, most punts don't want to be just far and straight. Most are some kind of situational play that calls for something special: directional punt out of bounds, work the wind, kick it toward the side of our best coverage player, take a little off it and drop it inside the ten-yard line. And that's exactly what our punter Josh Miller did. He lobbed a little wedge shot that we downed at the Eagles' six-yard line. The Eagles got it there with no time-outs left and ran a couple of low-percentage plays, and after a desperation pass that Rodney Harrison intercepted, we were champions. No Vinatieri magic, no Hail Marys, no big, splashy performances. Just winning plays.

How many times have we seen this? Play a seventeen-game regular season, two playoff games, and fifty-eight minutes of the Super Bowl, but everything comes down to that final situation, or two, or three. Often piled on top of each other, but all distinct, and all calling on months of careful prep work. Now imagine all the situations we practiced for that never came up.

The reason why situational football is greater than the sum of its parts is because, fundamentally, situational football is a way to practice adaptability. You might consider yourself to be a nimble thinker who can keep up with evolutions and contingencies in your field, but unless you practice that way of thinking, you'll never really know until it's too late. I like to put my players in somewhat challenging or complex situations in order to simulate real games, where circumstances will be outside of their control, requiring strategizing about complicated scenarios that forces them to imagine the game from all sides. It's a way of getting reps as a leader, almost like how militaries will assemble and practice maneuvers in semi-scripted war games.

Embracing situations means embracing change. In fact, it forces it.

"What's my role?" I often got this question from players at the start of every year. The player could want more playing time, or want to be used in a certain way. "What's my role?" may not be a simple question, but there's a simple answer. Each player's role on the team was determined by his performance. All I could do was evaluate what I was seeing and make decisions in the best interests of the team. That was my job. Each player had to earn his role every year—no one was entitled to a position, just like victories in the NFL have to be earned.

The more things you can do well, the more value you have to the team. If you can do only one thing, you better be able to do it exceptionally well. Somebody is going to have to do multiple jobs during a game—or at least be ready to. We can't operate on the assumption that everyone is always going to be available and will never need a backup. Your ability to do multiple things gives you tremendous value.

At the Patriots we had numerous examples of starting players who could do their primary jobs and also do other jobs to help the team. Players who could play multiple positions gave the coaches great game-planning flexibility and comfort. Players like that have tremendous value and led to us having a major advantage over many opponents who didn't have multitalented players or schemes to accommodate them.

I had the good fortune to have some great assistant coaches and many of them went on to become head coaches: Nick Saban, Kirk

Ferentz, Pat Hill, Dante Scarnecchia, Romeo Crennel, Al Groh, Scott O'Brien, Woody Widenhofer, Rod Dowhower, and Joe Judge, to name a few. Jim Schwartz, Charlie Weis, Brian Daboll, Brian Flores, Matt Patricia, and Josh McDaniels started coaching in areas that didn't end up being their specialty before they became head coaches. Weis, Daboll, and McDaniels started on defense, Patricia started on offense, and Schwartz and Flores started in scouting. Nick Caserio, Ozzie Newsome, and Phil Savage are examples of NFL general managers who were on my coaching staff early in their careers. Versatility is an important component for a successful team. Versatility and knowledge of other areas on the team will help prepare you for more responsibility.

TOOLS TO HELP

These days, technology can and should assist us in identifying key situations in advance and simulating circumstances beyond our control. Technology in football is sometimes misunderstood, by both its opponents and adherents, but it's simple to understand when we use it for the right reasons. As we discussed earlier, we humans are very good at thinking about all the first and tens in our lives—the predictable and dependable and commonplace events in front of us—and responding to them. We are less good at imagining far-off events and wild swings of fortune. For me, technology can help in the decision-making and preparation process, but it cannot replace a human. We need the human element to factor into football decisions.

Technology doesn't share our human bias toward the familiar, because technology itself is always advancing and adapting. The way we analyzed the game when my career began is unrecognizable compared to how things are today. The sheer volume of information available to us is beyond anything my father would have ever seen, and the ease of processing all that information is astounding. Sometimes it's overwhelming. I know I have been in football for a long time, longer than most, but methods of gathering information and studying it have come as far as anything in any other aspect of my life. To be clear, I'm not complaining. There are some downsides, of course. For instance, a lot of what you read and see on social media is stupid. High-definition game film, available instantly, is not. Don't get so frustrated by the former that you fail to appreciate the latter. I've always been ready for the information-gathering and -processing parts of my job to be quicker. Believe me, it used to be a grind.

For example, here's how I studied situations my first year in the league with the Baltimore Colts: I wrote every play in our system onto an eight-by-ten-inch card, and then I registered on the outside edge of each card every situation in which we might deploy the play: first and ten, deep in opponent territory, screen pass, need four yards to convert, etc. However many of those situations applied, I'd mark each on the play card. Then I'd take out my hole puncher and punch out a hole next to each scenario I'd written down. There must have been a hundred holes around the edge of some cards by the time I was done. Once you had a whole stack of cards, you'd slide an ice pick into one specific hole that was associated with a specific scenario—let's say, third down—and boom, all the relevant cards would drop out. Need a screen pass? Stick the pick in the screen hole and all the screens fall out. When I looked at all the screen passes, I would put the results on the "Screen Breakdown." This breakdown would tell us how many were strong side, how many were weak side, how many were to the halfback, how many were play-action, how many were third down, how many were second down . . . okay, got it. Back into the pile. I would do a hundred breakdowns—screens, third downs, inside-the-five plays, inside-the-ten plays, slot runs, slot passes, play-action, and so on. Every week, the coaches would add a couple extra breakdowns, so the group of plays grew all year. (By the way, I'm not kidding about the ice pick. It was an actual ice pick. It probably didn't pass OSHA regulations, to be honest.)

That's as primitive as you can get: the ice pick method. It would be like today's teenagers using rotary phones or record players. But it worked. Situational football: tagged, punched, collated, like we were etymologists looking at a thousand specimens in a museum somewhere. I don't know how we had enough time to actually practice with all the paperwork we were doing.

Today we just point and click on whatever situation we want, using our software that costs a hundred grand a year, and we've got whatever we need instantaneously. Unless of course there's a glitch in the technology or we're working remote and there's a problem with Wi-Fi or the server connection.

I do worry that some new technologies, especially those that are outside the game (but play a major part in the private lives of our players), have stopped pushing the ball forward on innovation except in new ways to cut corners. There are a hundred new gadgets every season that are going to save the day. I am all for technology that helps us avoid things like ice picks and hole punchers. But the point of the time-saving should be that it *permits us to work more,* not to work less. Especially in a game where margins make all the difference. You have to understand: if you have the technology, so does your rival. If you saved time by instructing a chatbot to compose fifty email pitches, your competitor used it to compose five hundred. Technology lifts all boats (at least those boats that aren't too stubborn to make use of it), which nets out to zero impact on winning. Unless you use the technology to help yourself work more, and work harder.

Throughout my career as an NFL head coach, every year before the start of training camp, I required each player to pass a conditioning test. This was part of their annual physical exam, to show they were physically ready to compete. The test was a series of twenty sprints of varying distance and time requirements, based on player position—wide receivers and defensive backs were required to do their twenty sixty-yard sprints in under eight seconds, while linemen had to run their twenty forty-yard sprints in under six seconds.

The task was simple: you didn't practice until you passed the test. For many players, this became a source of great anxiety. You might be surprised to hear that NFL players experienced stress over a running test that would be very familiar to a high school gym student, but it's true and it happened every year—inevitably, a handful of players either didn't stay in good enough shape during their vacation or cut water weight the day before their run test in order to meet their official weight, ensuring they were dehydrated all day. Many struggled, and many *knew* they were going to struggle.

Which means they'd try to get out of it. After a few years of hearing all kinds of reasons why players couldn't participate ("My back hurts from the long flight to Massachusetts . . . Can I not run?") I decided to get ahead of all the excuses. A month before the test, I'd remind players that the conditioning test was not about speed. Conditioning is about *work*. There's no pill you can take, no shake you can drink, and no gizmo that can do the work and switch your body into playing shape. But we're living in the "work smarter, not harder" age. Tom Brady, one of the slowest quarterbacks in the league, never had any trouble with the test. Went twenty for twenty. Mike Vrabel ran his conditioning test with the defensive backs, just because he wanted to, and because he knew he was in condition (and it was probably a little flex on his part). But Mike was never a speed player. He just worked. Bernie Kosar was certainly not fast, but he always aced the conditioning test.

Technology has nothing to do with any of that. Virtual reality glasses, animated opponents up on a screen, analysis of wind speed and how many feet the ball will be affected kicking in a certain direction at Gillette Stadium . . . I've seen or been pitched a lot. None of them take the place of work.

It's the same with data analytics. Statistics have been part of football my whole life; we used them before they had a name and a full department in the organization. If I need a software engineer to tell me the Jets' offense passes the ball 80 percent of the time out of a certain personnel group or formation, then I shouldn't have a job coaching football. My eyes should be enough to tell me it's 80 percent. An 80 percent trend is meaningful. But if it's closer to a 60/40 situation, I'm most likely not making decisions off that anyway. Big, obvious things should be big and obvious to you. Small, piddling differences, visible only to some software, simply don't matter that much, especially in football, where we have relatively few games. I'm sure the piddling differences add up when you simulate one hundred thousand games on Madden, but we don't live in a computer. We live in a world where small differences can be overcome. Overcome them with work.

FIND DIFFERENT
WAYS TO WIN

Your skills, your career, and your organization are going to grow as you start to win. That will mean that some coworkers and colleagues who you once clicked with will be left behind or, more optimistically, spin off and begin their own winning journeys in the circumstances that are right for them. A winning career is not necessarily a stable career, and may indeed look relatively chaotic from time to time. As a leader, you have to accept that personnel change is value neutral. But this is possible only if you have established certain permanent factors and created an intelligible culture that any new faces will know about in advance and be expected to join without hesitation. Once you have established the core of a winning organization, you will be able to add and remove pieces with confidence.

Charlie Weis was the right offensive coordinator for the infancy years of Tom Brady's career with the Patriots. He kept things relatively basic without being predictable, and worked with a less dynamic corps of skill players than what our roster would have a few years later. (Our offensive results from the early 2000s looked almost nothing like our offense from the 2010s, even though it was the same quarterback running the same foundational system.) Finding wins was his—and my—full-time job. He did it well.

Then, in 2005, he was hired to be Notre Dame's head coach. It was a major change for me, our coaching staff, and Tom. But it soon became clear that Josh McDaniels—nearly the same age as Tom— would be the perfect person to take over. In 2002, Josh had replaced Brian Daboll on defense, and prior to the 2004 season, I moved Josh to the offensive staff to coach the quarterbacks under Charlie. As with other situations involving coaching changes, Charlie did a great job of preparing Josh to work on offense. When Charlie left for Notre Dame in 2005, Josh took over as the play caller and essentially became the offensive coordinator. Josh is the son of a football coach, and he was a mathematics major, a real example of all-around intelligence. If he hadn't gone into coaching he'd probably have made just as big an impact on whatever company he was directing.

CHANGE

No one person makes a culture, but they can come close.

I learned a lot about change as an eighteen-year-old. I played center for the legendary high school coach (and Maryland Hall of Famer) Al Laramore. Football could not have been any simpler. Anyone who played for Big Al will remember our four plays. The three runs were: 22 Power, 24 Quick Trap, and 28 Counter. And our pass play was Sprint Right (or Left). Our blocking assignments were: (1) block man on, (2) no man on, block first man inside, and (3) no man inside, block across to first linebacker. The offense couldn't have been any simpler, and we ran two defenses: Gap 6 and Split 6. They were basically the same. The linebackers would line up in the A gaps and the tackles in the B gaps on Gap 6. On Split 6, the tackles and linebackers would switch gaps.

Above all else, we stressed fundamentals and execution. We practiced the same four offensive plays over and over and over and over.

One year later, I played postgraduate football at Phillips Academy in Andover, Massachusetts, under Coach Steve Sorota, who became a perfect example of how to maintain a singular, successful culture while adapting to changing circumstances. In his case, the changing circumstances had less to do with note cards and iPads and more to do with basic notions of life and liberty in America. In his forty-two years at Andover, he coached through wars and social upheaval, and by the time I arrived, a new shift was on the horizon: teenagers were starting to understand themselves as a cohesive social group, something more than kids, and they felt adults needed to respect them. Sorota knew this and soon became a legend for the way he approached his team. Many stories recall a relatively soft-spoken coach—not a shouter, not a drill sergeant—who never tried to push the uppity kids back into their pigeonholes.

For me, the change between Coach Laramore and Coach Sorota could not have been more dramatic. Our quarterback at Andover was also a postgraduate. Milt Holt, from Honolulu, was an elite athlete with all the skills and charisma you want in a quarterback. Milt was an accurate lefty passer and an elusive runner (he had to be elusive with me blocking in front of him)! In Coach Sorota's system, the quarterback called the plays—a far cry from Big Al, who called every offensive play with messenger guards. The two coaches had very different styles—but both styles were successful. This taught me a great lesson: embrace change. If you have a good plan, and consistently follow it, you have a chance for success regardless of what comes your way.

When *The New York Times* interviewed him in 1954 (identifying him as a "former Fordham star"; he played there with Vince Lombardi and the Seven Blocks of Granite) about the upcoming season opener against Worcester Academy and his still-undecided game-day roster, he replied simply: "You see, this will be our first week of comprehensive practice. Our first six days were devoted to fundamentals. Last week, it was difficult to do much because classes began and students were busy taking the usual opening-week examinations. This week, there's nothing to stop us."

A week for fundamentals. I love it. The most important thing to know is that Andover beat their archrival Exeter that year, 31–6, to complete an 8–0 season. Certainly nothing stopped us that day.

I bring up Sorota as an example of how culture and change can comfortably exist together, and as a leader you have outsized influence on how to manage that relationship. By all accounts, Sorota established a caring, serious, and thoughtful culture of refinement in his program throughout the most dramatic decades of the twentieth century, and delivered numerous wins against Exeter. I hear plenty of coaches from different sports and leagues, and plenty of businesspeople, complain about the rapidity of social change and how it is making their lives as coaches more difficult. I feel confident saying that Sorota and Andover weathered more fundamental changes to society—and to the pool of young men from whom he composed his teams—than any of us living and working today.

ADAPTABILITY TRUMPS UNCERTAINTY. NEW TECHNOLOGY AND IDEAS ARE GREAT AND CAN ENHANCE A PROGRAM, BUT YOU CAN EXPECT THAT YOUR COMPETITORS WILL HAVE THE

SAME GOOD TECHNOLOGY THAT YOU HAVE. USE TECHNOLOGY TO CUT TIME AND ENERGY, AND REDIRECT THE SAVINGS INTO PRODUCTIVE WORK THAT WILL RESULT IN VICTORIES.

FIFTEEN

CULTURE

Somewhere, someone came up with the phrase "the Patriot Way." I think they made some money off it. Good for them.

Here's something you should know: the Patriot Way does not exist. I assume the phrase started circulating after our first two Super Bowls; people were scrambling, trying to find some kind of explanation for what they were seeing. Tom Brady wasn't Tom Brady yet. He wasn't breaking every record and routinely dissecting defenses from the pocket. Our identity was still up for grabs. At least it was in the outside world.

Inside, we didn't have a "way." We had a culture. One that happened to work. We built it in collaboration with our players, instead of forcing something onto them. The culture was a commitment not only to play the right way but to a personal code, a doctrine that aligned with our goals as a team.

Before I get into what our culture was really all about, I want to get something straight. It'll seem obvious, but I'm not against obvious. Obvious can be good. (Remember, part of our culture is based on simple statements communicated over and over again.) So here's some obviousness: culture didn't make the game-saving stop on third and one late in the 2001 "Snow Bowl" against the Raiders. Tedy Bruschi, Ty Law, and Richard Seymour made that stop. Culture didn't call our offensive touchdown in the 2002 Super Bowl. Charlie Weis did. Culture didn't sack Matt Ryan when he had the Falcons in field goal range to make it a two-score game with less than four minutes to go in the 2017 Super Bowl. Trey Flowers did. Culture didn't pressure or intercept Rams quarterback Jared Goff while driving to tie the 2019 Super Bowl. Duron Harmon and Stephon Gilmore did. Culture didn't give every Patriots player, coach, and fan belief that any game, no matter the score, was winnable. Tom Brady did.

Culture doesn't do things; culture creates the circumstances under which *people* can do things. Culture prevents individuals from rationalizing cutting corners. Culture helps people think of themselves as defenders and stewards of a mission or an outlook, and encourages them to carry it over to the next generation. Culture binds and culture grows. And it couldn't be simpler to implement.

It starts at the top. This is unavoidable. Leaders have to set the tone.

In 2003, the Patriots had the number one seed in the AFC, but we knew that a showdown against the Colts was looming. The Patriots defeated the Colts in the regular season, but they had scored 34 points against us. The Colts scored 447 points in the regular season and 79 points combined in their playoff victories over Denver and Kansas City. They were absolutely stacked on offense. They had four Hall of Fame offensive players: quarterback Peyton Manning, running back Edgerrin James, and the wide receiver pair of Marvin Harrison and Reggie Wayne. They also had several other top players like tight end Dallas Clark, center Jeff Saturday, and left tackle Tarik Glenn.

The Colts offense was directed by Manning, who rarely huddled. Manning ran the offense from the line of scrimmage. Preparing for the Colts was hard because of their elite talent and Manning's ability to control the offense. We tried running the Colts' plays in practice, but we needed to practice their plays based on what Manning would do. Damon Huard, our backup quarterback, knew our defense from all the plays he'd run against them all year. So, for championship week, Huard ran the scout team and prepared our defense in the best way possible. We defeated the Colts, 24–10. Our defense was outstanding in limiting the great Colts offense to only ten points. Damon Huard had a lot to do with how well the defense played. He earned a game ball and he didn't even play in the game. That was our culture. Damon did his job to help his teammates play well.

I've always wanted our culture to be simple enough to be boiled down to a few basics. I want it to be learnable—and teachable—in seconds. Like I said earlier, we don't need culture to do anything. We just need it to exist and to be able to be activated in the minds of everyone in the building. It serves the same function as, say, the title of a book. The real stuff is inside, and it'll take work to read, to interpret, to understand, and to implement in your life—but the title you can grasp in a second.

To put a clear, simple culture into effect, I had some help from the operations staff. After all, they were the ones who knew how to cut and hang foam board. Upon my request, they hung a sign up by a glass entrance door to the facility. Nothing fancy, no glitzy LED lights or digital readouts. Didn't matter if the Wi-Fi went out or if some piece of software needed updating; that sign could have been hung up by Bear Bryant. When you entered the facility, you read four lines:

DO YOUR JOB

WORK HARD

BE ATTENTIVE

PUT THE TEAM FIRST

And, when you left the facility, the opposite side of the sign read:

IGNORE THE NOISE

MANAGE EXPECTATIONS

SPEAK FOR YOURSELF

DON'T BELIEVE OR FUEL THE HYPE

The location was key and intentional. The sign wasn't in the locker room or weight room or somewhere else dominated by the players. The words weren't supposed to be motivational. Instead, the fundamentals spelled out on the board were meant to be understood as descriptions of our expectations, for everyone in the organization to see whenever they entered or exited the building. If everyone followed through on all those things, our culture would flourish. If that wasn't the case, I would have had to create a new set.

Compare what I'm saying with the image many fans (and some coaches) have in their minds of locker room theatrics. The decisive moment when a coach or team captain delivers a speech that finally nails the "team culture" and gets everyone on board and believing they can win. Then they rush out to the field and who knows what happens. Maybe they win, maybe they lose. It'll certainly have nothing to do with the speech they just heard.

If you're trying to establish a culture in the locker room, you are several months (if not years) too late. You'd have a better shot at reading a dictionary to study for the LSAT. It's not happening. Put the cameras down. Stop rehearsing stuff in front of a mirror.

Our culture was treated like it was a piece of furniture in the facility—always there, and always relied on. Every day. Not just during the season, not just on game days. It was there for us to see, and any time any of us was falling behind or coming up short, it was a place to land as we prepared ourselves to stand back up.

One day, you will be responsible for establishing a culture. Until then you are responsible for upholding and living up to the culture of your organization. Let's see what that looks like.

ON THE WAY IN

As coaches, we didn't go into games against Houston defensive lineman J.J. Watt telling the offensive linemen, "We won't be able to move the ball unless we block J.J. Watt . . . now you go figure out how to do it." Putting accountability and action on just one person never works out well. Instead, we would spend days on Watt, imagining every run scenario in relation to his position on the field, and then we had to reimagine them in the event that one of our starters got hurt. That's team football. No player should ever be on their own, especially when they're up against one of the best opponents they'll see that season.

It's the same with culture and our couple dozen words. I didn't put a small handful of words on a sign and leave it at that. They were useful only after I'd gone over exactly what they meant, again and again. How they applied to the week, the opponent, or that year's team. If we hadn't constantly reinforced the meaning of the messages, then they would have just been wallpaper, faded into the background by whatever was on people's phones on the way to their locker or desk.

So we made it clear:

DO YOUR JOB

The key thing here is to keep the phrase open-ended. It's not "Did you do your job?" It's not a question. "Do Your Job" is *always* doing it. It also means not trying to do someone else's job (you won't do it as well as it needs to be done, and you'll also be enabling the other guy to get lazy). We all have job descriptions. You know what your job is. I know what mine is, and so does everyone in the organization. We all have more than enough to do before we have to start thinking about what other guys are doing. If everyone focuses on what they're asked to do, we'll be better off.

WORK HARD

Working hard doesn't mean showing up early and leaving late. If all you're worried about is creating a production out of producing, then you're not working hard (plus, the need to show off probably means that you're not really doing that much to begin with). We all have the same amount of time, but it's how we spend it that can make the difference. In the early days, our culture developed a kind of mutual accountability based around half-joking callouts.

If a player or staff member left the building at 7 p.m. while others were staying later, the early departer might get a text message along the lines of "Oh, working a half day today?" This was before we established some guardrails around our work/life balance, but I can't say it wasn't effective. In the old culture, the paranoia that went along with "Am I not working as hard as everyone else?" was very, very real. We knew that we could get an edge by how we worked. We talked all the time about outworking and out-preparing our opponents, which consisted of focusing on the things that would make a difference: Hit the important targets. Don't waste time on things that are minor. Study your opponent to find keys into what he might do next.

BE ATTENTIVE

This one is simple: pay attention to all the details associated with your job. Make an effort to learn everything the coaches are teaching you. Don't just do your job; understand all aspects of it. Day to day, only you know the potential impact you and your role can have. If you aren't attentive, then it's only a matter of time before everyone knows how inattentive you are. And they won't be happy about it. Being attentive + working hard = improvement. This was a pillar of our culture. Every day was about improvement. You cannot improve without the knowledge of *how* to improve *and* actually doing something about it by working hard.

PUT THE TEAM FIRST

I would need several more books to cover the many examples I have of players sacrificing individual glory for the greater good. The best one is Rob Gronkowski. Gronkowski stands out in stature and performance; he's an all-time great. But there is one thing Gronk is incapable of. He can't "blend." His style of play, what he could do, his personality (and that's even before we get to his celebrations), didn't resemble anyone else's. And he didn't try much to change that.

Tight ends don't typically get paid extra for blocking. There's no financial incentive for playing the role of sixth offensive lineman or blocking fullback. The number of times Gronk sacrificed what was best for him—which was to get the ball in his hands—to block in the running game, or to help as an extra pass protector, is beyond anything I could count. I'm certain that 100 percent of the time Gronk would have preferred to be away from the scrum of three-hundred-pounders and out in a part of the field where he was a physical mismatch. But I can't point to one instance when he complained or lobbied to be used as a glorified wide receiver, which many tight ends tend to be. Never once did he give off an impression of "I'm here to catch passes and score TDs, not to block defensive ends." He knew his job description, but he always was looking for ways to add to it.

In Put the Team First, there's only one team and only one culture. I've heard of plenty of organizations that allow for several competing cultures to grow, whether they be specific teams or entire units. For us, there was no "defensive culture" and "offensive culture." We were all subject to one overriding culture. Subcultures are just engines for contradiction and chaos.

A football team is made up of a team of teams: kickoff team, third-down offense, dime defense, and so on. The idea is to get everyone to work together or, to put it another way, play what we call complementary football. That means that each unit works in conjunction with other units, and collectively, the team benefits when everyone does their part.

Understand this is not a lecture on selflessness. The path to individual reward and recognition is through the group succeeding. Nobody should want to be seen as the best player on the worst team, or the most productive worker at a bankrupt enterprise. No more than wanting the most attractive home in the worst neighborhood. We're far better off being one cog in a high-functioning machine.

I know you've heard people say, "Nope, not in my job description" a few times. Some people seem to relish saying it, like they're about to pull out their employment contract, point to this or that clause, and get an A-plus for accuracy—and on paper, they may be right. But those people don't contribute to a winning culture. They are annoying. They are losers. When it came to what was best for our offense, the word "no" wasn't in the great Rob Gronkowski's vocabulary. And that doesn't just trickle down. It overflows. If your All-Pro, Hall of Fame player has that attitude, how can others not? It's part of what made him, and us, great.

This last principle, Put the Team First, was really the umbrella principle to the "On the way in" mindset. We probably said it out loud more than any other—and we enforced it accordingly. There was no way to get around it.

If you walked into a meeting late, there was going to be a problem unless you had a good reason and it was expressed to me in advance. I set the tone on this early on. In my very first meeting with the team, during our spring workout phase in 2000, one of our starters walked in five minutes after the meeting started and sat down in the front row. I couldn't believe it—I felt like he was daring me to do something. Normally, if a player was late, he would come into the meeting through the back entrance, as inconspicuously as possible. I stared at him when he sat down. . . . He returned my glare with an "Is something wrong?" look. I threw him out of the meeting on the spot along with some profanity-laced remarks.

In 2001, the night before our season-opening game, we were in Cincinnati (why does it always seem to come back to Cincinnati?) when, on the eve of his first career start, a player was late for the meeting. He and a couple of teammates had decided to go shopping for special boots in Kentucky, just on the other side of the Ohio River, but unfortunately for him—and us—the bridge traffic didn't care about our game-day schedule. He was late getting back to the team hotel, and I had to sit him. I was not particularly sympathetic. He hadn't put the team first. He'd put boots first. Shopping, a jammed-up bridge, and lateness were a bad combination in our culture—and certainly not a formula for winning. That was the first and last time that problem came up with that player, who went on to start for a decade, and did, after all, live by our culture and help us win.

LIVING AND BREATHING CULTURE

Enough about the slogans. Culture lives and breathes. It takes oxygen. It takes *people*.

Dante Scarnecchia is a huge reason why the Patriots experienced two decades of unprecedented victory. He was one of the best offensive line coaches in league history, and I can easily draw a direct line between his coaching, Tom Brady's success, and our team's success. Dante coached fifty-nine players during my time as Patriots head coach, more players than any other position coach, and I am certain all of them knew they were being coached by the best. Dante had thirty-six seasons in the NFL under six different head coaches. He has said the two easiest to work for were Parcells and me. Maybe his six years of service in the US Marine Corps Reserve had something to do with it; or maybe, as he often told me, it was that our expectations for everything were always absolutely clear. All you had to do was go and do it. Easy. Chalk it up to foam signs and simple slogans.

Dante's "MFings" were part of the culture. I could never put many of the things he screamed into guys' faces into print, but you can use your imagination. Whenever those confrontations occurred (and they were legendary, given that Dante is about five eight and the guys he was pushing around were twice or three times his total size), teammates accepted the harsh language because he was good and because he always pushed them in step with the overall expectations of the team. The culture he created made it okay for him to be, let's say . . . feisty. His players knew that stuff came out because he had their backs. Dante absolutely helped his players play better and reach their potential. He loved them. I would call it tough love, and similar to my dad. His players loved him too.

I know the world is wired in different ways in 2025 than it was in 2005, or certainly in 1975, my first year in coaching. Some good, some bad. Some just annoying. Now we can't go two days without having to meet a quota on positive reinforcement. We have to promote sufficient workplace harmony. We have to dole out praise all the time. If it's not clear, I struggle with these kinds of things. If there's exceptional performance, if someone goes far above and beyond to help us win, then I'm all for recognizing it. It's one of the best parts of the job. But just doing what you are supposed to do shouldn't get you a celebration. It's the culture. It's the baseline. It's how things are supposed to work. Without those things in place, will we lose? Of course. But simply putting ourselves in a position to *work to win* doesn't warrant a celebration. That's what we get paid for. It's what Dante got paid to do for thirty-six years.

Culture cannot be carried over from one organization to another, or forced. It's all organic, not transferable. But there's a reason why people like Steve Jobs and Jack Welch have been celebrated for their management, even when it seems so tied up in their respective companies. Apple is probably the single most unique major company in the world, and GE doesn't even exist like it once did under Welch. But people still seek out their wisdom, and I think most of those people are looking for guidance on the question of culture.

A leader can try to implement his own approach, but if it's not in sync with his employees (i.e., if he or she doesn't know how to hire the right people), then those efforts are dead on arrival.

One person can't create or sustain culture, but if anyone could, it would have been Tedy Bruschi. His last name was music to Patriots fans' ears, but Tedy was beloved more for being the quintessential champion. His full-tilt, emotional-yet-intelligent style of play was contagious, and even the most casual fan could tell he carried himself like a winner. He had as much passion for football, the team, and winning as any player I've been around—the ultimate culture builder.

It started from the beginning. A six-foot, 250-pound defensive lineman at Arizona, he switched to linebacker to make it at the next level in the NFL. Tedy was a great teammate, never made excuses, and was never afraid to speak up and say what needed to be said to make our team better. He challenged his teammates, his coaches, the media, our opponents, and me. He was a joyful warrior, and he thrived in tough conditions. During my nine years coaching Tedy, he earned forty-six game balls, the most on the team. (If anyone in NFL history beats that record in a nine-year span, please come forward.)

One of my favorite moments with him was in the immediate aftermath of our 2004 playoff win over the Colts. This was during the heart of the Patriots–Colts rivalry, on and off the field. We had beaten them in the 2003 AFC Championship game, largely thanks to our outstanding defense, which had roughed up Peyton Manning and his dynamic group of skill position players. And then that offseason, the NFL Competition Committee, led in part by Colts General Manager Bill Polian, established a strong emphasis on reducing contact by defensive players. We all found it very interesting. This was one in a long line of "Patriots Rules" that took hold during our run of success.

Fast-forward to the 2004 playoff game, when we stuffed the Colts' vaunted offense even more thoroughly than in the 2003 game, new rules and everything. On the field right after the game ended, Tedy found the first microphone available, from ESPN, and unleashed one of the greatest, most jubilant postgame rants ever.

"You come to Foxborough, it's going to be snowing, it's going to be cold. Come on in here.... You want to change the rules? Change them. We still play. And we win. That's what we do."

Still warms my heart to this day. Tedy wasn't talking just to a reporter. Or just to the Colts or the NFL. He wasn't speaking to anyone in particular. He was speaking to *everyone*, about his pride for the Patriots culture and *his* culture of winning. It was a fun chirp with an edge, a middle finger with a smile. And an affirmation that our culture was the place to be. Too many people tried to depict our culture as being all about discipline, accountability, and subordinating yourself to the greater good. I mean, they were right about all that. What they failed to add was that those things lead to winning, and winning is very, very fun indeed.

A month later, out of nowhere, Tedy had a stroke at the age of thirty-one. He was dealt a frightening and debilitating hand at the peak of his career and his life as a husband, father, and champion, but, as with everything he did, Tedy dealt with this life-altering challenge head-on. During his rehabilitation, he asked his doctor to help connect him with other athletes who had come back from what he had, so he could see how they handled it and understand what to expect. (Unfortunately, the doctor told him there were no solid precedents.) Eight months later, on one of the most emotional nights of my career, he was back on the field making seven tackles against the Buffalo Bills. He was named the 2005 NFL Comeback Player of the Year. He became a true engine of our culture, taking it in, making it work, and showing everyone else what it looked like to be going at full power.

"Any person that thinks he's above anything isn't going to fit in, and they're not going to last. If we think there's a guy like that, we're going to let you know about it. We've had that talk with a lot of guys."

Fifteen years after his retirement, he had this to say about tough coaching: "Think of a wet towel, okay? You know, a wet towel when it drips and what you tried to do was get all of that water out of that wet towel, and how do you do it? You take both of your hands and you wring that towel over and over and over again, okay? That towel is the player. Bill Belichick is the hands that wring the water out, and the water is the talent of that player. Bill Belichick could get every drop of physical ability, mental ability, football-playing ability out of you somehow, some way, and it didn't matter how he did it, it was going to happen. . . . Because the success of winning Super Bowls is what this game is all about."

A lot of that wringing isn't much fun. Culture isn't just for special moments and triumphs. It's not just for when you get near your breaking point and need to dig deep to keep going. Part of the power of a culture, and a signal that it's fully implemented, is that it's ubiquitous. It's on the signs, it's in the huddle, it's in meetings, it's how workers talk to each other and pick each other up. Players who complained, quit, or lamented about this or that unfairness to the media were easy to spot. Our culture was about embracing the struggle. Practicing for two and a half hours and then running the conditioning hill was tough. So were the extra meetings and getting called out. Players and assistant coaches having in the back of their minds *What's the head coach going to think about what I'm about to say, or already said, in the media?* was annoying. But we were all in it together. That's how a team handles it, with the realization that losing is a lot worse.

In his first year coaching the New Orleans Saints, Sean Payton gathered his staff and outlined the culture he was trying to build. It would be defined, he explained, by details, work, and unselfishness. And then he told each position coach to identify one player from their previous team who best fit that new criteria. Those were the guys he wanted to try and get on their team. Three years later, the Saints were champions. The perfect sequence: he had a vision, he communicated it clearly, and his team executed it. No time or breath wasted. And it was all about finding the right people for the vision.

Culture guides decisions, but it can't be static. There's establishing a winning culture and then there's maintaining it. Both are difficult, but one leads to the other. It requires new people, new leaders, new workers, which then attract more people, leaders, and workers with the good results the culture has produced. Our first generation of winners motivated the second generation.

Edelman, McCourty, Andrews & Co. didn't win just because they wanted to but because they *had* to. They understood the standard and expectations, but they also grew tired of hearing about the Patriots' championship era and of my habit of breaking out film on "how Harrison did it . . . how McGinest did it . . ." They wanted to be the ones on the How To reels for future teams. One of the things that I'm proudest of is how tightly the first-generation Patriots held on to the culture and continued preaching it and rooting for the next generation. They passed it along and protected it.

Many of our retired players still tell me they find themselves using the same principles and words we used in team meetings. They talk to their children about doing their job, teamwork, and dependability. Since 2005, the foundation Tedy's Team has raised nearly $10 million for stroke research and education programs. If you've been in a truly elite culture, it stays with you too. It carries you through any endeavor. Tedy embodied our winning culture more than anyone and still does.

ON THE WAY OUT

Our culture didn't stop at the doors to the facility, and that old foam sign made that clear. When you left, you were confronted with four additional expectations: Ignore the Noise, Manage Expectations, Speak for Yourself, and Don't Believe or Fuel the Hype.

As you can see, these expressions are a little more specific than the rules you read on your way in. That's because our culture had a purpose. And that purpose existed off the field just as much as it existed on it. Yes, players were free to conduct their lives as they saw fit (as long as they stayed healthy and ready) once they left the facility, but I didn't want them to think of our culture as something they switched on and off depending on where they happened to be at any moment. What your expectations will be for your culture as it extends out into the "real world," past the doors of your office or jobsite, will be up to you. Even the most laissez-faire managers have some expectations of decorum for their employees, but I would encourage you to find ways to link these basic expectations back to a positive and forward-thinking culture. Cultures are resilient because people want to be a part of them. The more you associate your expectations with a culture, embed them in a culture, and hire people who make that culture seem joyful and focused on winning, the more buy-in you will get from everyone.

I learned about culture as I grew up around the Navy football team. Michael Connelly wrote a book about the 1963 Navy football team titled *The President's Team*, which refers to the relationship between the team and President Kennedy. Connelly writes about the remarkable unity of this group, and how they remain a close-knit family sixty years later. The impact on me of seeing this culture was immense. As a head coach, I tried to pattern my teams on the real-life example that the 1963 Navy football team had provided.

I heard my father say many times that Admiral Tom Lynch, captain of the '63 Navy team, was the best leader he ever saw. That statement carried a lot of weight with me. I used Tom's leadership model of "ship/shipmate/self" as a blueprint for my philosophy of team building, but I modified it slightly: put the *team* first, then your *teammate*, and finally, your*self*. That would be my model for the team, starting with the head coach. In retrospect, putting the priorities of the football team ahead of ownership goals ultimately led to a fractured relationship in Foxborough.

Get the right people on the team who are all committed to the same goal. Every member of the team earns respect from every other team member each day through their effort to help the team and their teammates. Our team in 2001 had a culture that most closely approximated what I saw from the 1963 Navy team. Team, teammate, self.

I won my last Super Bowl with the Patriots in February 2019. It was an odd time for the team: all our winning had brought celebrity and publicity like we had never seen before, which meant the media was running with "storylines" about how hard things had been, how we coaches all had gotten too demanding, and how any feeling of fun had left the building.

To be clear, there had always been some level of conflict and stress—and there always will be with a football team. That wasn't the issue. The issue was the leaks. There had been a time when everything, good and bad, stayed in-house. We would trade for a player and nobody would know until the guy was in the building, ready to go practice. No longer. The media was more than willing to run with any story they got, and after a few of them, I inferred that some of this leaking was coming directly from the players.

It wasn't a catastrophic situation, but we were in the middle of a season in which we had serious expectations that we would win. No one had time to monitor people's behaviors or attitudes, and even if we had, it was unclear how we could handle it. And then, one day, on a blank whiteboard in the hallway, someone wrote three words: "Winning Is Fun." No one came forward as the anonymous author (the handwriting was supposedly very evocative of a certain former Kent State quarterback) and we all moved on with our lives. It was not some decisive moment in the season, but it made me smile. In the midst of struggle, someone in the organization had identified the need to remind everyone of what they were working toward and taken a definitive stance. I was proud that, even as we neared the end of a run, the culture persisted, and the guys who most embodied it made sure that it would not be forgotten. There will always be people who might not fully buy in, and they will be easier to replace. And those who do buy in will carry you forward when it matters most.

YOU MAKE THE CULTURE, BUT WINNING MAKES IT STICK. CULTURE CANNOT EXIST WITHOUT PEOPLE TO UPHOLD IT. A GOOD, WINNING CULTURE CAN WITHSTAND PLENTY OF ADVERSITY IF IT'S CONSISTENTLY PRESENT.

A GOOD SIGN IS WORTH ITS WEIGHT IN CARDBOARD. WE ALL EARN RESPECT FROM EACH OTHER BY OUR EFFORTS EVERY DAY. EACH OF US NEEDS TO DO OUR JOB WELL AND PUT THE TEAM FIRST.

EPILOGUE

After forty-nine years of telling people how to do their jobs, this book has finally afforded me the opportunity to tell you how I did my job, and to share some of the lessons I have learned from my life in football. I cannot really tell you how to do *your* job, but I wanted to convey how I dealt with all kinds of situations, the good, the bad, and the ugly, and how, through all of it, my central and overriding focus has been on the team. Your focus should also be on your team.

The definition of a team, according to the *Cambridge English Dictionary*: "a number of people who act together as a group, either in a sport or in order to achieve something." Even in football, a team is about something more than a roster, a uniform, and a mascot. A team is more than the people who make it up. My definition of a team would be something like this: a team is an ecosystem of people working together to accomplish a goal. We are all part of some team, some ecosystem. If you think you aren't, you're wrong. And you're probably failing to do your job.

Long before I became a head coach, I learned the centrality of the team concept while running (and crawling) around the facilities at the University of North Carolina and then by observing my father and other great coaches at the Naval Academy. From those experiences, I have carried the question "What can I do to help my team win?" through my entire life and career. I hope with this book I can help you develop ways to work harder, be more attentive, put the team first, and achieve more and more success in the lifelong pursuit of doing your job.

Finally, I assume that you can tell from this book that I love football! When you love what you do, a job doesn't feel like work. Coaching football does not feel like work for me—I love all aspects of the job, including writing about it, as I have done here. I took joy out of writing every chapter in this book, and I truly love to coach. Sure, there have been some tough days along the way, but I have always tried to embrace the process. I have learned from every player I coached, every coach I worked with, and all the support people across seven different organizations. The joy of coaching, learning, and working with people committed to the same goal will never get old for me.

After forty-nine years in the NFL, and one year in the media, I am . . .

On to Chapel Hill.

ACKNOWLEDGMENTS

No matter how many games or championships I won, they were never perfect. The perfectly played or coached game didn't happen and never will. Similarly, any individuals I list in appreciation for making this book possible—which really means making my career possible—warrant more than a two-word entry. Collectively, they made me, as did countless others who deserve mention.

Thank you to my long-standing teammate and friend Berj Najarian.

Thank you to my literary Dream Team of InkWell Management and Simon & Schuster, Michael Carlisle, Richard Pine, William Callahan, Jofie Ferrari-Adler, and Jonathan Karp.

Thank you to my idea mill and creative muse, Jordon Hudson.

Thank you to the Navy players, coaches, and staff who inspired me: Jon Batchelor, Tom Belichick, Joe Bellino, Vice Admiral Sean Buck, Vice Admiral Ted Carter, Jack Cloud, Bo Coppedge, Jack Connolly, Lee Corso, Dick Duden, Rick Forzano, Chet Gladchuk, Wayne Hardin, John "Hoppy" Hopkins, Ernie Jorge, Tom Lynch, Joe Mark, Phil McConkey, Chet Moeller, Phil Monahan, Terry

Murray, Brian Newberry, Ken Niumatalolo, Ray Novelli, Tom O'Brien, Red Romo, Roger Staubach, John Stufflebeem, Elliot Uzelac, George Welsh.

Thank you to all our servicemen and -women for defending our freedom. Thank you to the members of the US Navy, Navy SEALs, and Blue Angels who have helped me lead and develop men.

Thank you to all our police officers and firefighters who protect us.

Thank you to my confidants from across sports. Bruce Arena, Paul Assaiante, Charles Barkley, Keegan Bradley, Bruce Cassidy, Ryan Clark, Neil Cornrich, Billy Donovan, Terry Francona, Mike Fratello, Jim Gray, Kelly Amonte Hiller, Jimmy Johnson, Claude Julien, Bob Knight, Sol Kumin, Tony La Russa, Joe Mazzulla, Jim Montgomery, Bill Perocchi, Dave Pietramala, Rick Pitino, Paul Rabil, Pat Riley, Doc Rivers, Jeff Saturday, Alex Stern, Brad Stevens, Rudy Tanzi, Joe Torre, Acacia Walker, Jerry York. Your advice and wisdom for coaching, leadership, and winning are priceless.

Thank you to the icon Jim Brown. For a new, young head coach at the Cleveland Browns, you graciously taught me about winning and managing players, and, most indelibly, you opened my eyes to a segment of society I had never experienced. Your impact on me, on young people, and on the world transcends and far surpasses your legendary status in the athletic arena.

Thank you to the elite NFL competition who forced me to work harder and be a better coach. Thank you, Troy Aikman, Pete Carroll, Tom Coughlin, Bill Cowher, John Elway, Dwight Freeney, Tony Gonzalez, John Harbaugh, Chad Johnson, Patrick Mahomes, Eli Manning, Peyton Manning, Sean Payton, Ed Reed, Andy Reid, Aaron Rodgers, Mike Shanahan, Ron Wolf, and so many other legends who got me up each morning and kept me awake every night.

Thank you to Chris Berman, Gil Brandt, Paul Brown, Casey Coleman, Al Davis, Roger Goodell, John Madden, Wellington Mara, Jim Nantz, Ken Rodgers, Pete Rozelle, Ed Sabol, Steve Sabol, Pat Summerall, and Paul Tagliabue for making the NFL a great league.

Thank you to my college and high school teammates and coaches who guided and put up with me: Jim Akin, Bob Bianchi, Buzz Bissinger, Jock Burns, Dave Campbell, Chris Carter, Vinnie Colelli, Dave Cronin, Andy Darpino, George Davala, Bill Devereaux, Peter Donovan, Dave Durian, Jim Farrell, Tom Foley, Mark Fredland, Bob Frisbee, Dennis Harrington, Dick Hart, Matt Hoey, Milt Holt, Rob Ingraham, Terry Jackson, Bill Kirby, Larry Leonard, Pat McQuillan, Bob Mekeel, Ronnie Pastrana, Jim Plato, Tom Price, Tom Tokarz, Brad Vanacore, Sam Walker, Dave Whiting, and many, many others.

Thank you to the incredible coaches and staff who showed me the way and who acquired and developed our championship-level people and players: Ernie Adams, Dom Anile, Jim Bates, Maxie Baughan, George Boutselis, Tom Bresnahan, Joe Bugel, Moses Cabrera, Jimmy Carr, Nick Caserio, Joe Collier, Romeo Crennel, Brian Daboll, Jimmy Dee, Thomas Dimitroff, Rollie Dotsch, Whitey Dovell, Rod Dowhower, Jack Easterby, Ivan Fears, Kirk Ferentz, Jedd Fisch, Brian Flores, Jerry Glanville, Al Groh, Matt Groh, Pat Hill, Joe Judge, Bucko Kilroy, Joe Kim, Pat Kirwan, Linda Leoni, Jason Licht, Michael Lombardi, Ted Marchibroda, Chris Mattes, Richie McCabe, Josh McDaniels, Nancy Meier, Red Miller, Richard Miller, Ozzie Newsome, Bill O'Brien, Scott O'Brien, Mike O'Shea, Monti Ossenfort, Matt Patricia, Dean Pees, Ray Perkins, Scott Pioli, Bob Quinn, Floyd Reese, Jon Robinson, Nick Saban, Phil Savage, Dante Scarnecchia, Greg Schiano, Jim Schwartz, Brad

Seely, Ken Shipp, Fritz Shurmur, Jerry Simmons, Brian Smith, Mike Tannenbaum, Rick Venturi, Charlie Weis, Woody Widenhofer, Mike Woicik.

Thank you to the hundreds of players who worked and sacrificed for the team, who sweat and bled, and who won games and championships: Ryan Allen, Danny Amendola, David Andrews, Joe Andruzzi, Kyle Arrington, Tom Ashworth, Carl Banks, Tully Banta-Cain, Mark Bavaro, Drew Bledsoe, LeGarrette Blount, Brandon Bolden, Tom Brady, Deion Branch, Orlando Brown, Troy Brown, Tedy Bruschi, Terrell Buckley, Rex Burkhead, Rob Burnett, Jim Burt, Adam Butler, Malcolm Butler, Marcus Cannon, Joe Cardona, Harry Carson, Matt Cassel, Matt Chatham, Je'Rod Cherry, Patrick Chung, Jamie Collins, Rosevelt Colvin, Mike Compton, Dan Connolly, Brandin Cooks, Bryan Cox, Don Davis, James Develin, Corey Dillon, Nate Ebner, Julian Edelman, Marc Edwards, Steve Everitt, Kevin Faulk, Christian Fauria, Trey Flowers, Randall Gay, Stephon Gilmore, David Givens, Aaron Glenn, Stephen Gostkowski, Dan Graham, Jarvis Green, Victor Green, BenJarvus Green-Ellis, Rob Gronkowski, Lawrence Guy, Bobby Hamilton, Duron Harmon, Antwan Harris, Rodney Harrison, Dont'a Hightower, Ellis Hobbs, Russ Hochstein, Damon Huard, Byron Hunt, Larry Izzo, Michael Jackson, Dave Jennings, Pepper Johnson, Ted Johnson, Chandler Jones, Jonathan Jones, Tebucky Jones, Eric Kettani, Terry Kinard, Brandon King, Dan Koppen, Bernie Kosar, Sean Landeta, Matt Light, Chris Long, Rick Lyle, Logan Mankins, Leonard Marshall, George Martin, Shaq Mason, Jerod Mayo, Keenan McCardell, Devin McCourty, Jason McCourty, Willie McGinest, Sony Michel, Josh Miller, Lawyer Milloy, Stevon Moore, Joe Morris, Randy Moss, Steve Neal, Rob Ninkovich, Patrick Pass, Lonie Paxton, Roman Phifer, Anthony Pleasant, Tyrone Poole, Gary Reasons, J. R. Redmond, Steve Rehage, Darrelle Revis,

Elandon Roberts, Lee Rouson, Logan Ryan, Asante Samuel, Junior Seau, Richard Seymour, Phil Simms, Matthew Slater, Antowain Smith, Otis Smith, Nate Solder, Aqib Talib, Lawrence Taylor, Vinny Testaverde, Tom Tupa, Eric Turner, Kyle Van Noy, Shane Vereen, Adam Vinatieri, Sebastian Vollmer, Mike Vrabel, Everson Walls, Ken Walter, Ty Warren, Ted Washington, Benjamin Watson, Wes Welker, Ryan Wendell, James White, Jermaine Wiggins, Vince Wilfork, Perry Williams, Wally Williams, Eugene Wilson, Tavon Wilson, Deatrich Wise, Danny Woodhead, Damien Woody.

ABOUT THE AUTHOR

BILL BELICHICK is an eight-time Super Bowl champion. Widely considered the greatest football coach of all time, he is the only head coach in NFL history to win six Super Bowls, all with the New England Patriots. He is currently the head coach of the University of North Carolina football team, which his father also coached from 1953 to 1955.